Small Business Smarts

Small Business Smarts

BUILDING BUZZ WITH SOCIAL MEDIA

Steve O'Leary, Kim Sheehan, and Sterling Lentz

 PRAEGER

AN IMPRINT OF ABC-CLIO, LLC
Santa Barbara, California • Denver, Colorado • Oxford, England

Library of Congress Cataloging-in-Publication Data

O'Leary, Steve.
   Small business smarts : building buzz with social media / Steve O'Leary, Kim Sheehan, Sterling Lentz.
      p. cm.
   Includes bibliographical references and index.
   ISBN 978–0–313–39409–6 (hard copy : alk. paper) — ISBN 978–0–313–39410–2 (ebook)
1. Internet marketing. 2. Social media—Economic aspects. 3. Online social networks—Economic aspects. 4. Customer relations—Technological innovations. 5. Small business marketing. I. Sheehan, Kim. II. Lentz, Sterling. III. Title.
HF5415.1265.O44   2011
658.8'72—dc22   2011006345

ISBN: 978–0–313–39409–6
EISBN: 978–0–313–39410–2

15 14 13 12 11   1 2 3 4 5

This book is also available on the World Wide Web as an eBook.
Visit www.abc-clio.com for details.

Praeger
An Imprint of ABC-CLIO, LLC

ABC-CLIO, LLC
130 Cremona Drive, P.O. Box 1911
Santa Barbara, California 93116-1911

This book is printed on acid-free paper (∞)

Manufactured in the United States of America

To our families

Contents

Acknowledgments, ix

Introduction, xi

1
An Introduction to Strategic Social Media, 1

2
Online Listening: Monitoring Customer Conversations Wherever
They Happen, 13
- Getting Started with Blogging, 33

3
Building Relationships: How to Build Social Networks
and Engage Customers Using Social Media, 41
- Getting Started with Facebook, 63

4
Social Messaging: Best Practices for Social Communication, 71
- Getting Started with Twitter, 91

5
Say Goodbye to the Yellow Pages: Strategies to Optimize Search, 97
- Getting Started with Google Places, 113

6
Better than the Rotary: Using Social Media to Create
a Business Network, 115
- Getting Started with LinkedIn, 128

7

Media Metrics: Measuring the Effects of Social Media, 133

8

Social Media Audits: A Tool to Create Your Strategy, 149

Appendix, 167

References, 173

Index, 175

Acknowledgments

We gratefully acknowledge the support, wisdom, feedback, and insights from the following colleagues and experts:

- The small business people who shared their time, insights, and stories with us.
- Students in the J610 Social Media Workshop, part of the Master's Program in Strategic Communication at the University of Oregon, especially Mary Ann Albright, Heather McDaniel, and Jonathan Nelson.
- Tim Gleason, Al Stavitsky, Leslie Steeves, Deborah Morrison, David Koranda, and Harsha Gangadharbatla at the University of Oregon.
- Grabbing Green colleagues Eric Anderson, Michael Todd, and Carrie Lane.
- Author, colleague, and friend Lauren Kessler, for the opportunity to practice what we preach.
- Colleagues at O'Leary & Partners, especially Eric Anderson (again!), Tom Blinn, Chollada Buathong, Jaclyn Eubanks, Kaytee Irwin, Maria Migliore, Scott Penniston, and Shannon Walker.

Introduction

Everyone, it seems, is talking about social media. What was once the prevue of high school students has now become an important element in marketing plans for all types of businesses. Fast-food giants have pages on Facebook devoted to frozen drinks, grocery chains issue "tweets" about produce on sale, and car companies introduce their new television commercials via the online channel YouTube. However, it is not just the "big boys" playing in the social media playground. Many small businesses have also started social media marketing campaigns. Other small businesses are wary, and that is not a surprise. Social media is exciting, scary, intimidating, and empowering, all at the same time.

Where do you fit in? Are you ready to try social media? Do you use social media, but wonder how to use it more strategically? Maybe you need some convincing that social media is worth your time. If you fall into any of these groups, this book is for you.

We want to help small business owners like you become more successful and, as we say on our website, to help you grab some green! Our first book, *Building Buzz to Beat the Big Boys: Word of Mouth Marketing for Small Business*, discussed strategies and tactics for creating word-of-mouth campaigns in both the "real" and online world. In that book, we stressed the importance of listening to customers and finding the best ways to get them to talk about your business. Our second book, *Small Business Smarts: How to Survive and Even Thrive in a Recession*, discussed the challenges of marketing a small business in tough times. One of our key ideas in that book is the importance of continuing a marketing presence even when your budget is cut. The book you are reading now is the logical next step. We understand the importance of online communication for small businesses. And, through our recent conversations with small business owners, we saw how many wanted to learn more about online media, particularly about social networks.

Free social networks such as Facebook and Twitter are powerful tools to compete with "the big boys" (and their budgets), since they allow small businesses to compete on a relatively equal playing field with much larger businesses. Keep in mind, though, that even though these tools are free, they do have a cost: participating in social media requires time, organization, a willingness to try new ideas, and patience. Participating in the social media sphere also requires you to shift your marketing message mind-set from one-way messages to interactive conversations. While this may sound somewhat daunting, this shift can be much easier for you than it might be for a big corporation and their "corporate speak" that requires layers of approval to try something new.

Before we started this book, we created a series of action guides: short, easy-to-use manuals for small business owners looking to get involved on popular sites like Facebook, LinkedIn, and others. We received great feedback on these guides, but we also learned that small business people like you wanted to learn more. We realized then that we could better address all the issues related to social media with a book on the subject. To write the book, we enlisted the help of small businesses from across the United States and Canada, from an ice cream truck in Los Angeles to a boutique hotel in New York, and many more restaurants, florists, coffee shops, and auto repair shops in between. We know there is nothing like having one small business owner telling another about their experiences. That is what you will find in this book: real stories from real small business owners of how they have embraced social media.

We found these experts in several different ways. We started by talking to local businesses we patronize ourselves. We then asked friends, family, and colleagues about the small businesses they patronized. We searched Facebook and Twitter for active users and started following many businesses to see how they used social media. We sent out interview invitations via Facebook, Twitter, and email. Over the course of a year, we talked to people in person, over the phone, and over the Internet to get their insights. We used a standard interview guide, although our focus evolved to highlight different areas of the social media space.

Some businesses we interviewed were taking their first steps into social media. Others had been there for months (an eternity online) and were transitioning from a heavy traditional-media diet to leveraging the power of social media to lower advertising costs. Most of the people we spoke with learned how to use social media on their own, and their insights should reduce your learning curve so you can be interacting in the social media sphere very quickly.

Interaction is the essence of social media, and inside this book you will find the tools and resources you need to reach out to potential customers in the online places they spend their time. We start in Chapter 1 with basic definitions and a consideration of how goals can be set for your social media campaign. In Chapter 2, you will learn the importance of online listening for developing goals and strategies. Building and maintaining your social media community is covered in Chapter 3, and in Chapter 4 you'll learn about different types of messaging strategies for your social media campaign.

The more people use social media, the more likely they will be to use online searches to find businesses, so in Chapter 5 we discuss how to use the power of search. We recognize the importance of building not only a social network but also a business-to-business network in Chapter 6. In Chapter 7, you will learn about different ways to measure your progress and success in social media, and in Chapter 8, we will walk you through different types of social media audits so you can get an idea of the competitive landscape you are competing in, as well as set benchmarks for your future campaigns.

Along the way, we provide step-by-step instructions to starting a new account on a variety of popular social media sites, as well as specific strategies and tactics to build an online marketing campaign using social media. We recognize, of course, that every business will not (and should not) use every recommendation in this book. As you read this book, always consider your business. Social media is free, which is part of the reason it is so attractive to small businesses, but it can also be time consuming. We have organized this book to cover the most essential and popular social media websites, but even those, if tackled all at once, can be daunting.

Keep in mind that with social media, whether it is Facebook, Twitter, or Yelp, your goal should always be to provide a place for your customers to interact with your brand. Doing so requires constant participation. As you move through this book, take time to evaluate how your business fits into the social media picture. One size does not fit all. That's why we've included the insights of a variety of different business types. Chances are, there are one or two businesses similar to your own: meet our small business resources at the end of Chapter 1.

Since social media is an ever-changing landscape, this book and its recommendations will need updating. So, we propose that as you read this book, you go to our blog and share your own experiences. What you have done to date? What tactics have you tried, and have they been successful? What new social media are you using? Please visit our blog at http://www.grabbinggreen.com/blog and let us know how social media is working for you. One of our hopes with Grabbing Green has been to have small business owners share their experiences with other owners, whether it is about social media, improving customer service, or any other topic. So, we hope you will use this opportunity to share GrabbingGreen.com with other small business owners.

If you are not sure where to start, or even unsure about whether social media can be useful or not, this book is for you. There has never been a better time to begin using social media. Many of our recommendations are easy to implement, intuitive, and, based on the input from small business owners, effective. As you get started, remember the importance of research and to continue to listen to what your customers are saying about you, both in your business and online. They will provide feedback that will be more valuable to you than any social media expert can provide. As you move along, you will find that you will grow more comfortable with these new types of media that once seemed confusing and inaccessible. As you do, broaden your focus and explore, but always be sure to measure your success against past performance.

Good luck! We are about to embark on an exciting journey.

1

An Introduction to Strategic Social Media

I would say that we got into social media because there was a lot of people getting into it and we didn't want to be left behind. We wanted to see what it was about, see what it could offer to us, and make sure that we continue to have a brand that was thought of as cutting edge.
—Erica Leaf, Imagine Graphics

Social network sites have changed the face of the Internet. By becoming an essential part of people's lives online, sites such as Facebook and Twitter have redefined how people communicate with each other, and how businesses large and small communicate with their customers. With millions of people using social media everyday, it is no wonder that so many businesses want to be active and visible in the social media space.

Today, many large businesses believe that a social media presence is a necessity. Some businesses believe this is important just because everyone else is doing it, or because a "social media expert" said they would go out of business if they did not. Some are caught up in the numbers: Facebook reached the 500-million-profile mark in less than four years, and while Twitter is much smaller, active users total almost 25 million after less than three years. Others may want to join because they think social media is free marketing. The truth is, many businesses (regardless of the size or the industry) begin using social media without a clear idea of why they are using social media, and without any type of strategy or road map for success. As a result, their online presence flounders, they cannot attract an audience, and they give up and tell others that social media is not for them.

For many small businesses, social media is not even on their marketing radar. Many small business owners simply do not have the time or inclination to use social media for themselves, and so they do not think about using it for their business. A study published in April 2010 by Citibank reported that 81 percent of the 552 small businesses surveyed did not use any type of social media to promote their business (Citibank 2010). Interestingly, though, the business owners believed word-of-mouth marketing was the most effective way to promote their business. Clearly, many small businesses do not see how social media is the electronic version of traditional word of mouth.

There are other reasons why some businesses are not making the most of the social media opportunity. Maybe they are out of tune with what a social conversation online is like, and they are not taking the time to listen to what people are saying about their business. Or perhaps they are treating their social media efforts as distinct from their traditional marketing campaigns. Perhaps they are concerned about conversations that include negative comments about their business posted for all to see. Maybe they have not committed the time and resources to correctly implement social media. In most cases, it is probably a combination of some or all of these elements.

This book is a road map for your business's involvement with social media and for making the most of all your online activities. We have gone to the experts: small business owners who are currently using social media as an integral part of their word-of-mouth program. Based on our interviews with these businesses, we have designed this book to give you ideas on how to make the most of your online presence using social media.

What Are Social Media?

Andreas Kaplan and Michael Haenlein (2010) have defined social media as "a group of Internet-based applications that build on the ideological and technological foundations of Web 2.0, and that allow the creation and exchange of user-generated content." Essentially, social media are online sites that support and encourage interaction. Marketing messages turn from one-way, top-down messages into a dialogue between a brand (like your business) and a customer. This idea of interactivity differs from other types of digital messaging, such as banner advertisements.

Digital messages such as banner advertisements are interactive in that the goal is for an online user to "click" on the ad and be directed to a branded website. While social media messaging can be used for that kind of directional interactivity, the dialogue aspect is much more important, and can be much more effective in building a strong brand and a strong word-of-mouth program for your business.

When we think of social media, we specifically think of social networking services. A social network service has a goal to build and encourage social networks or social relations among people, often people who share interests, activities, or offline relationships. When your business is part of one person's network, your interactions with that individual can be seen by everyone in that individual's own network. What this means is that one individual's conversation can start a chain of conversations within that individual's social group or network. This can lead to positive word of mouth for your business.

There are many different types of social network services, but they all have some things in common. They consist of some type of profile or representation of a user and that user's social links, along with a way for communications to happen. Many social network services also provide additional services such as image and video sharing, e-mail, and instant messaging. Social networking sites allow users to share ideas, activities, events, and interests within their individual networks.

Dozens of online sites fall under this definition. For social network services devoted primarily to online communication, several major categories of websites exist. These include:

- Blogs: The term blog comes from the term "web log," which is a website that is generally created and maintained by an individual and that includes regular entries of commentary, descriptions of events, or other material such as graphics or video. Many blogs focus on commentary or news on a particular subject. Others more closely resemble personal online diaries. Blog entries are commonly displayed in reverse-chronological order. "Blog" can also be used as a verb, meaning to maintain or add content to a blog. People who read a blog can leave comments to which other readers and the blog's author can respond. Some popular blogging tools include WordPress, Blogger, LiveJournal, and TypePad.

- Microblogging is similar to blogging except the message size is constrained: microblogs often limit entries to fewer than 300 characters, resulting in brief messages. Microblogging applications also allow links to other websites. As we write this, the most popular microblogging site is Twitter. Other services include Jaiku, Plurk, Tumblr, Posterous, Yammer, and Qaiku.

- Social networking sites allow for multiple forms of communication between a user and his or her network. The most popular site at the time of this book's publishing is Facebook, but numerous other sites exist, including Google Buzz, Friendster, Geni.com, Hi5, LinkedIn, MySpace, Ning, Orkut, Skyrock, Qzone, Vkontakte, and Flirtomatic.

- Multimedia sites allow for sharing of photographic and video images. Users can tag and arrange content so others can search and find images. Photography- and art-sharing sites include deviantArt, Flickr, Photobucket, Picasa, SmugMug, and Zooomr; while video-sharing sites include YouTube, Viddler, Vimeo, and sevenload.

- Reviews and opinion sites allow online users to rate products, services, and businesses. Many retailers are reviewed on sites such as Yelp and Insider Pages.

- Geosocial networks: These are tools that use geographic services such as GPS to engage users who submit their location data to a service either through their computer or, more likely, through their mobile phones. Users can see where their friends are frequenting, and businesses can reward frequent visitors who "check in" at their location. Geosocial network programs include foursquare, Gowalla, and Bright Kite; information can also be integrated into other social networks.

Why are there so many different social media sites? Within a single category, some sites offer simple and streamlined tools and applications, while others offer ones that are more complex. Some appeal to younger people, some to older people. Some are brand new, and some have been around for quite a while. We focus the discussion in this book on the most used and most popular services in 2010, including Facebook, Twitter, Yelp, and YouTube. At the same time, we recognize everyone is looking for "the next big thing," and the landscape is always changing. Three years ago, MySpace was the hottest property online, and now most users have migrated to Facebook. While we cannot predict what the next hot thing will be, we do believe that the key ideas about connecting and engaging with customers cross media boundaries, and while the interface for the connection may change, the key ideas regarding the value and nature of conversations do not.

These sites tend to have their own terminology for the people who use and connect on the site. Throughout this book, we will refer to the people who are part of an individual's social network for a particular site as that person's "followers" or their "network." You will also see the terms friends and fans used at various social networking sites, but in order to simplify our discussions, we will stick to the terms followers and network.

Setting Goals

With so many social media choices, many businesses are overwhelmed and do not know where to begin. One important thing we learned from the business owners we interviewed is that there is no right or wrong place to start, and really no right or wrong ways to participate in the social network scene. The key is that you commit to participating, and this book will help you understand what that means.

One important first step, though, is to look at your own business goals and see how social media can be used to meet them.

- *Sales Goals*: All businesses have sales goals, and most businesses want to increase their sales. Chris Brogan (2009) suggests that social media can be used to make more people aware of your business. If increased awareness can lead to more sales, then that can be part of your social media goals.

- *Service Goals*: Many companies use social media to help with service. Social media can be used to quickly answer customer questions and direct them to places where they can find more detailed information. It also shows that your company is listening. If improved service is your goal, then social media can be appropriate for you.

- *Engagement Goals*: Engagement is a soft measure, unlike hard measures such as sales. But in today's cluttered and competitive environment, customer loyalty and trust is often the one point of differentiation that will bring sales to your door. Social media is exceptional for engaging customers, starting conversations, and deepening customer trust. The key to this is the idea of a dialogue: that you have ongoing conversations and interactions with customers in order to build customer loyalty.

As a small business owner, it is likely that you are used to setting goals for your business, particularly in terms of sales, customer counts, service time, and the like. Setting social media goals is similar. It is best to follow the SMART methodology: in effect, goals should be specific, measurable, achievable, realistic, and timed.

- *Specific* means that your goals and objectives are concrete, detailed, focused, and well defined: it is clear what you want to see happen once you have implemented your social media plan.
- *Measurable* means that there is a mechanism in place that will let you analyze your progress and know when your goal is achieved. (See Chapter 7 for more detail on measurement of social media.)
- *Achievable* means that that the goals and objectives can be accomplished given the resources you have available in order to keep you motivated through the process.
- *Realistic* means that the goals and objectives fit in with the other priorities for your business.
- *Timed* means that there is a sense of urgency in achieving the goals and objectives, in that there is a specific time frame to accomplish what you want (Ambler 2006).

Learning from the Experts

There are many self-stylized social media experts who blog regularly about the "right" ways to do social media. Our point of view is that the best experts for small businesses are the people who are in the trenches doing social media every day and actively creating the definition of a social media strategy. To write this book, we reached out to small business owners using all types of social media. We sought to represent a range of businesses across North America: from small, one-person operations to larger businesses that were still independently owned and operated. Some businesses have only one person involved with social media; others have an entire staff. What they have in common is that they are interested in social media, they all believe it can have a beneficial impact on their business, and they know there is no right or wrong way to succeed in the social media world. Throughout this book, they provide a wealth of ideas for you to consider and test for your business.

Please meet our small business owners and managers whose insights helped to create this book:

- Mark Beauchamp is the owner of Café Yumm! a small chain of fast-casual restaurants in the Northwest. Along with his social media expert, Kelli Matthews, Mark is using social media to build a strong community of good-food lovers for his restaurant.

- Jillian Bisinger and her husband, Tony Zucca, operate Jillian Bisinger Modern Photography, based in Los Angeles. Jillian and Tony update their blog daily with pictures of the wedding and family sessions they photograph, and now use social media to direct potential clients to the blog and to connect with other service providers.

- Beth Colla and Tim Ferguson own the "mobile ice cream parlor" Lake Street Creamery. Following the popular food-truck trend in Los Angeles, Beth and Tim created a gourmet ice cream truck that changes locations daily. They used social media to generate interest and excitement in their business before they even launched; now they use social media to alert customers where the truck will stop each day.

- Dan Bohan is the owner of WW Windows, a window installation company based in the Bay Area of California. Dan uses search engine optimization to increase referrals through his website.

- Adam Cuppy is the creative and online media director for Dutch Bros., a chain of drive-through coffee stores located throughout the Western United States. Dutch Bros. prides itself on a high level of personalized customer service, and Cuppy sees social media as a way to extend the customer experience to the online world.

- Somer Deck recently was in charge of marketing for Fifth Street Public Market, a small shopping area in Eugene, Oregon, where independent stores sell a range of goods. Somer and her staff promoted events at the market with the goal of making a visit to the market a family event.

Social media both encourages followers to join in the fun and cross-promotes events at the different stores.

- Rich and Kim Gans are the husband-and-wife team that owns Sweet Flour Bakery in Toronto, Canada. Their social media goals are to connect with customers and make them feel that the bakery is a special place where they are part of the family.

- Lisa Hartwick owns Hartwick's Kitchen Store, a specialty store in the Northwest. Her social media goals include building her online presence to create more awareness of in-store promotions and events. She also strategically uses social media for special sales offers.

- William Kennedy is the general manager of CD World, a successful independent record store. The social media goals of CD World include announcing in-store events with traveling musicians and promoting new and special releases that are available only at CD World.

- Erica Leaf is vice president of Imagine Graphics, an Oregon company that designs and produces signs, banners, and trade show graphics. Leaf's social media goals are to connect with customers and keep them informed of what the company is doing and how they are growing, especially important given what they produce is an infrequent purchase among their customers.

- Brian Mason, owner of the popcorn company SKP-Popcorn (http://www.skp-popcorn.com/) is a relative newcomer to social media. SKP's popcorn is grown in the company's home state of Indiana, and they are the official popcorn for Lucas Oil Stadium (home of the Indianapolis Colts). The company plans to use social media to build a larger network that will lead to increased sales for the online side of the business.

- Della Mendenhall manages the family-owned Gillespie Florist in Indianapolis, Indiana. Della sees social media as an important tool to drive customers to both the store and the store's website.

- A veteran restaurateur, Paco Miller owns Tia Juana's Long Bar and Grill in Irvine, California, and Tia Juana's Beach Cantina in Maui, Hawaii. Paco has used social media for several years, and now focuses on Twitter and text messaging to attract customers to his restaurants and nightclubs.

- Patty Miller owns the Tattered Cover Bookstore in Denver, Colorado, one of the most successful independent bookstores in the United States. Patty uses social media to promote local events and to connect their audience with new releases.

- Brad Niva is the owner of Rogue Wilderness Adventures, a rafting, fishing and hiking outfitter in the Rogue River area of southern Oregon. Because his is a destination business, he focuses primarily on optimizing his search to attract customers looking for a rugged vacation.

- Trey Pitsenger owns the Golden Gecko Garden Center in Garden Valley, California, and uses his blog to discuss the nursery industry with hundreds of interested nursery owners from around the world.

- Daniel Pollard is webmaster at the Pelican Pub and Brewery in Pacific City, Oregon. Facebook engages patrons of the pub online, which is important given that the pub is located in a vacation spot, and visiting it must be a "destination" choice rather than a spur-of-the-moment decision.

- Janice "JP" Poloway is a nutritionist, guide, and social media expert at Mountain Trek, another destination marketer with "boot camp" programs in Canada and Baja California. JP uses social media to keep her past customers connected and to give new customers a feel for what their program at Mountain Trek would be like.

- "Utah" Dave Robison is a realtor based in Salt Lake City, Utah. His goal with social media is to connect with customers, prospective customers, and other realtors through his home page, blog, and Facebook presence.

- Justin Stobb owns All Wheel Drive Auto in the Seattle area, a garage that specializes in repair of Subaru automobiles. Justin sees social media as a way to promote himself and his staff as experts in Subaru repairs.

- Robbie Vitrano is the chief branding and design officer for a new chain of pizza restaurants called Naked Pizza. A rapidly growing business, Robbie uses social media to generate interest in new locations and judge the viability of alternative locations.

- Adam Wallace is the marketing manager of the Roger Smith Hotel in New York, and works with his assistant Brian Simpson to promote this art-centric, New York–based hotel. The hotel's social media efforts in Facebook, YouTube, and Twitter, and on their blog, are designed to develop positive word of mouth and customer comments for the hotel, which in turn lead to future reservations and loyal customers.

- Jesse Yu is cofounder and director of brand development for a small chain of yogurt stores called Qoola in Vancouver, Canada. Qoola uses social media to distinguish their fresh yogurt treats from the powdered yogurts found at other yogurt stores.

We have also been following the Facebook messages and tweets posted by dozens of other businesses, and learned much from this experience. The businesses we cite in this book include:

- The Bleeding Heart Bakery in Chicago, Illinois
- Blue Moon Burgers in Seattle, Washington
- Burke's Bar in Yonkers, New York
- Hotel Lucia in Portland, Oregon
- King Estate Wineries in Oregon
- The Laughing Planet Café, based in Portland, Oregon
- Marche Restaurant in Eugene, Oregon
- Naples Tomato in Naples, Florida
- Sierra Trading Company, based in Cheyenne, Wyoming
- Southwest Airlines, based in Dallas, Texas

Getting Started

Perhaps you're one of those small businesses that aren't yet using social media, and want to learn how. Perhaps you have dabbled in social media with a personal account, and are ready to expand it for your business. Or perhaps you're looking to take your social media presence to the next level. We think regardless of your level of expertise, you'll find ideas in this book that you can get started with right now. We start in Chapter 2 with a discussion of online listening: how to find out what customers and others are saying about your business. In Chapter 3, we'll show you how to pick the "nerve center" for your business and to build your online network. Chapter 4 discusses the types of messages that you can consider using. In Chapter 5, we'll talk about optimizing your web presence for search engines. Chapter 6 addresses an under-discussed benefit of social media: to connect with other businesses who can help you build your own business. Chapter 7 outlines simple ways to measure your success. In Chapter 8, we'll share key tips on moving forward with social media.

Interspersed with these chapters are something we call "action ideas"—step-by-step instructions to get started with and use the leading forms of social media. These are good resources for those people who have never tried out social media. Additionally, at the end of each chapter, we share what we think are the best next steps for you, regardless of your level of expertise in social media.

We wish you success with your journey, and look forward to hearing your success stories.

2

Online Listening: Monitoring Customer Conversations Wherever They Happen

We get a lot of people who just love Café Yumm! And what I tell our managers and the owners is the criticisms are more important than the compliments. We get a lot of compliments. We get a lot of people that love it but they're saying, "We like the way you're doing things." What those compliments are not saying is here's what we don't like. Here's what you're not doing well. So the criticisms actually show you how to improve. And one of my core principles is constant improvement. Continual improvement. One small step at a time.

—Mark Beauchamp, Café Yumm!

People are social creatures, and spend a lot of time talking to each other. You already know that. But did you know that some studies show that each individual has at least five conversations about brands every day? These conversations have a huge impact on decisions people make every day.

As a business owner, you have the opportunity to interact with your customers, to know what they like (or don't like) based on what they choose to purchase. You also have the opportunity to start up a conversation if you want to learn more. These conversations are invaluable, but they're just the tip of the iceberg. There are hundreds of other conversations happening all the time online that can directly and indirectly affect your business in major ways. These conversations happen at social media sites like Facebook, they can happen in short bursts on Twitter, and they happen at online review sites like Yelp.com, which exist solely to allow customers to rate and review businesses. Combined, these conversations can raise your business above the competition just as easily as they can sink your business.

The key to social media listening is to embrace hearing both good and bad things about your business. While it is sometimes hard to do, hearing and reading negative comments about your business is one of the best ways to improve what you and your employees do every day, whether it is your service, your merchandise, or your interactions. Of course, you cannot control what people say about you, and about what has already happened. What social media does, though, is give you the opportunity to hear what you could not hear before and to start to address what needs addressing.

Listening to these conversations, both online and offline, is the foundation of social media strategy. Without it, you won't know who's talking about you, what they're saying, and how you might best influence them and those who are listening in. In this chapter, we'll discuss the importance of monitoring online conversations, how to respond to positive reviews, and how to turn negative reviews into a competitive advantage. Finally, we'll mention several online tools that will make listening a cinch and help you to locate influential voices online.

Why Listen?

Listening takes time, but there are many good reasons for you to commit to taking the time to listen to customers.

People Rely on Each Other's Opinions

People talk about brands all the time: about a great new product they found, a good deal at a favorite store, or a bad experience that they had with a salesperson. It's likely that every so often, one or two of these conversations have to do with your business—your brand. Most importantly, people trust each other's opinions more than they trust most other types of messages. You need the ability to be alerted quickly to the conversations people are having, both good and bad, about your business.

You might think that having a Facebook page or a Twitter feed is enough, and that your presence among the followers of your social media sites will give you a good idea of the conversations people are having.

However, these conversations are just one piece of the social media pie. There are people who are customers of your business who don't follow you on any social networking site and who aren't part of your email list. These people are blogging, tweeting, and updating their Facebook status, and if you aren't following them, then you won't know what they're saying.

Additionally, the social media world has many other types of sites, such as user-review sites, where people can talk about your brand. Justin Stobb (All Wheel Drive Auto) finds that he gets new customers at his repair shop from five-star reviews at various review sites. At some of these sites, you're welcome to join in the conversation, but again, you need to know where these conversations take place. We call this action monitoring the social web, and it is important to do this in order to know what people are saying and to respond to any negative comments as they come up.

Find Where Your Customers Are

Maria Ogneva (2010) described consumers who use social conversations as ways to help them make decisions as "social customers." The social customer learns about products, brands, and businesses through social channels and trusts her network to provide information to her. The social customer also expects brands to be present and involved in the same places where she is. Social listening helps you identify the social network sties where your customers and prospects spend time, and can help you devise a strategy for building your own presence there.

Tap into Opinion Leaders

Monitoring the social web gives you insights on who the "opinion leaders" are in your community. Social media guru Chris Brogan calls these people "trust agents," online identities that people trust as you would trust a friend, to give advice about products and services (Brogan 2009). In your geographic area, these trust agents may be bloggers: people who keep a regular online journal that online users can easily access. Many cities have local bloggers (potential trust agents) who are read by large numbers of people (more potential influencers and customers): Some of these people may be popular bloggers because they have columns in newspapers or shows on TV, but most have built their popularity from just being interesting, funny, or controversial. The *New York Times* dining blog, for example, is read by thousands of New Yorkers. In Omaha, Nebraska, five individuals contribute weekly to a blog about local restaurants. Bloggers in other cities focus on fashion and nightlife. Ask your friends, family, and employees what blogs they read to learn about your town, and start paying attention to what those bloggers are saying. Before you know, your finger will be on the pulse of your community.

Additionally, knowing the opinion leaders in your community gives you the opportunity to cultivate relationships with them and potentially generate positive word of mouth. You can invite opinion leaders to your business, or send them coupons to try something that you offer. They may or may not come visit your business, and if they do, they may or may not blog about it. The important thing to remember is that you have to go out and find these influential people; you need a plan to monitor the social web. To find them, you must monitor the social web.

Monitor the Competition to Gain an Advantage

Active online monitoring of what people are saying about your competitors can also help you gain an edge. You'll know what they're saying about themselves, how they're engaging the online community, and what people are saying about them. You then have the opportunity to tailor elements of your business in direct response to weaknesses you have discovered in your competitors.

> **2.1 Action Idea:** Track what people are saying about one or two of your direct competitors on a site like Yelp.com. This can give you insights into what you can say about your business that might attract more customers into your store.

Monitoring the Social Web

You might be saying to yourself, "I 'Google' my business on a regular basis; shouldn't that keep me in the loop?" What Google does not do well is keep track of the thousands of tweets and updates generated by sites like Twitter and Facebook. If all you do is Google your business, you will miss this key information. So in addition to paying attention to your own social media sites, it might make sense to consider changing your strategy to include other sites and tools specifically designed to get information about online conversations in order to prepare to monitor the social web.

If you have a Facebook page or a Twitter feed, you probably check them regularly to see what people are posting and saying about your company. This gives you a good overview of part of the conversations that are happening. In addition, many different sites exist that will help you on your quest to learn what people are saying about your business. There are three broad categories of sites: monitoring services, opinion/user-review sites, and specialized search engines.

Monitoring Services

Monitoring services allow you to use key words and terms that describe your business and to receive regular updates about conversations that include those terms. For instance, if you own a pet store, you might use the name of your company and the terms "pet store," "pet supplies," and "dog food" in your search. Once you've selected your terms and provided them to the monitoring service, the sites filter all the content passing through the web and—like a net—catch just the pages and information you're looking for.

One popular service is Google Alerts (http://www.google.com/alerts): you provide terms or keywords that interest you, and you'll receive email alerts when new content containing the terms is found. The limitation, as we've discussed, is that Google doesn't search all areas of the Internet equally, and some social media sites may be missed.

Other monitoring services include sites like Social Mention (http://www.socialmention.com), which monitors conversations happening on sites like Facebook and Twitter. Updates are delivered daily via email: for many businesses, this might happen every day. A good practice is to take 5 or 10 minutes when you get this email and quickly click on the links provided so you can read about your business at the actual site where the commentary occurred. In this way, you'll understand the complete context for the mention. When you receive an email, always take a few minutes to click on the links provided so you can place each mention in context. Creating these alerts takes minimal effort up front, but most of your time will be spent sorting through the email alerts for the conversations relevant to your business.

User-Review Sites

Opinion or user-review sites are websites where consumers can post reviews about a specific business, product, or service. These sites are important: ratings and review sites influence consumer shopping behavior. Reviews are generally started by a customer: for example, someone visits a coffee shop, logs onto a review site afterward, and posts a review about their experience. Most reviews are written by customers who have either a very strong positive experience or a very negative one, and research shows that those who have had a negative experience are 10 times more likely to talk about it (Sernovitz 2006). Google your business name, or category, along with the word "review" and you will get an idea on the number of review sites available.

Some popular businesses can have hundreds of reviews; newer businesses are likely to have fewer. Don't let the idea that some people may give your business a negative review put you off. Later in this chapter, we'll show you how to respond to negative reviews. Remember, also, that many businesses have so many positive reviews the negative ones are lost in the noise.

Review sites can also serve as a way to provide information about your business. Some review sites allow businesses to pay for enhanced listings: these allow you to post information about your business, such as your opening and closing hours and your locations. These enhanced listings do not affect reviews and ratings on the site; put another way, paying for an enhanced listing does not mean you have control over anything people are saying about your business. We think this is a good thing: you do not want to control comments. You need to hear what people are thinking and writing so you can address the concern, and possibly turn a negative reviewer into one who will write a positive review in the future.

Your business may be listed on several review sites, so you will need to spend a little time looking at the range of sites and determining your tactics. Generally, you'll find that the reviews start converging on one specific site that you can spend time focusing on. Here are some top sites for you to visit.

- Yelp (http://www.yelp.com) is one of the leading online sites for local business reviews. You can quickly and easily search for your business name and then see a list of what people have posted on the site about your business. Your review, out of five stars, will also appear in a list of Google results, which makes Yelp an extremely powerful influencer. You can also go to your business's competitors. Simply go to the Yelp site, enter the business name in the search box, and see what comes up. Yelp also allows you to set up a business account, which will allow you to:
  - Receive an email alert whenever a review is posted
  - Respond to comments
  - Provide special offers for Yelp reviewers
  - Allow you to post links to Yelp reviews on your own website
- Insider Pages (http://www.insiderpages.com) is neck-and-neck with Yelp in terms of popularity for learning about local businesses. Like Yelp, Insider Pages was created to help people find the best local businesses through recommendations from their friends and neighbors. Millions of people visit the site each month. You can also set up a business account: search for your business, and then click on the question that asks, "Are you the owner?" Once you claim your business, you can:
  - Add pictures to your site
  - Feature coupons

According to Brian Niva (Rogue Wilderness Adventures), sites like Yelp are becoming search engines within themselves. Both Yelp and Insider Pages frequently come up on the first page in Google searches: that is, if someone searched for "Italian Restaurants in Boston," it is likely that two of the top results will be the Yelp and Insider Pages for Italian restaurants. As you will read about in Chapter 5, this fact is a great reason to get your business reviewed on these sites.

There is one big difference between these two sites. If someone reviews your business on Yelp.com but has not written a review previously and does not review another business within about a month from the review of your business, Yelp will delete their review. Yelp's rationale is that the review might be from someone within your business, or someone whom you have paid to write the review. Insider Pages has no such policy as of this writing.

Here are some additional sites to check out:

- Angie's List (http://www.angieslist.com/) is a review site for service businesses, and currently allows consumers to rate a range of businesses. Angie's List is unique in that it charges members to use the site, both to post reviews and to read reviews. Reviews are also not anonymous. The site allows companies to respond to any criticisms posted on the site, similar to Yelp. They also allow businesses that receive good ratings to advertise on the site.

- Trip Advisor (http://www.tripadvisor.com) is the world's largest travel community and an international review site for hotels and local attractions. The site is filled with user reviews, and reviews often stimulate conversations between reviewers. Managers and owners can also register for their hotels and other properties and respond to review son the site

- Viewpoints.com (http://www.viewpoints.com) features a very easy search interface that can quickly show you many reviews on a specific category (such as shoe stores). You can filter reviews by normal settings (highest/lowest rated, most reviewed) as well as by demographics of reviewers. So, for instance, a fuel-conscious car shopper can see which vehicles were most reviewed, highest rated, or lowest rated by like-minded consumers.

- Google Places (formerly Google Local Business Center) lets you create a free Google page for your business that will appear in a list of local results at the top of a page of organic search results on Google. We provide complete directions on using Google Places following this chapter. Yahoo offers a similar service.

If you own or run a restaurant, a wealth of online sites are available to help you find out what people are saying about your eatery and your competition. Here are several you should check out:

- Urbanspoon (http://www.urbanspoon.com) features lots and lots of reviews from critics and diners—the richest source we've found. Additionally, anyone can update facts about the restaurant (i.e., the opening and closing times, types of food, and online contact information). If you're looking for online influencers, this is easily the best place to find them.

- Zagat (http://www.zagat.com) rates restaurants all over the world. Go to the site and enter your city (or even your street address) to find reviews. Even the little town of Eugene, Oregon, had listings for several restaurants with user reviews. Be sure to check the date to make sure you're getting the most recent scoop. Business owners can submit photos and menus: look for the link in the lower left-hand corner to set up a business account.

- Where the Locals Eat (http://www.wherethelocalseat.com) is a site geared to helping people who visit a city find good places where, um, the locals eat. The site is not very interactive from an owner perspective, as owners can only email any corrections to the information listed.

If your strategy is to keep on top of reviews and to be able to respond and react in a timely manner, you should plan to spend a few moments every day checking out the conversations happening about your brand. You now have a great opportunity to monitor the conversations about your brand. If there is a comment about your business that needs a response (such as a specific positive or negative comment), look for some type of mechanism (like Yelp has) to provide a response.

Social Media Search Engines

Social media search engines are similar to sites like Google, where you input search terms, keywords, or phrases and receive a listing of sites for you to visit. If you use Google to search about your business, you might be a bit overwhelmed with the number of results and wonder how to find the information you need. Using a different search engine helps to give you more precise results. Here are a few to consider:

- Keotag (http://www.keotag.com) does keyword searches across several different social networks, and it allows you to select the specific social network that you'll search. Keotag searches the big sites like Facebook as well as small social networks you might not have heard of, such as Newsvine or Bluedot. This tactic might generate some surprising results you've never seen before.

- YackTrack (http://www.yacktrack.com) is another social media monitoring tool that lets you search for comments on your content from various sources. If you make a comment on a blog, for example, you can use YackTrack to find other people who are commenting on the blog and then decide if you want to rejoin the conversation to share more information. Just simply enter the URL of the blog and then see what's happening there. What's even better is the "chatter" feature, which lets you enter a search term (like the name of your business) and then YackTrack searches through Friendfeed, Blogger, WordPress, and other blogging sites to see if people are talking about your business. This is a fast and easy way to keep up with conversations.

- Another search engine that focuses solely on blogs is BackType (http://www.backtype.com). At BackType, the engine indexes online conversations from across the web and posts them based on recency. You can enter the name of your business, your competitor's business, or your category in the search box on the front page, and the most recent comments from blogs, news stories, and other online sources will appear. So if your competitor is having a big sale, and you want to see what people are saying about it, this search engine provides the most recent information you can find on the web.

These search engines look through online communities that are text-based (also known as bulletin boards):

- BoardTracker (http://www.boardtracker.com) searches those text-based communities known as "bulletin boards" where people gather to talk about topics of interest to them. There are literally thousands of such boards, and keeping up with the conversations is somewhat of a challenge. A simple search box lets you search for your business, your category, or your competitors. The search box is clearly indicated on the home page. The name of the board where the conversation occurs is clearly identified, so you can see if there are boards that you should decide to follow on a regular basis.

- Boardreader (http://www.boardreader.com) also searches online communities, videos, and more. There is a simple search interface, and a great trend indicator that shows how popular the search term is. Boardreader is particularly helpful if your business provides a technical product or service, as these types of things are most commonly discussed on online forums with other knowledgeable users.

Here are two ways to monitor what is happening on Twitter:

- The Twitter search engine (http://search.twitter.com/) is a quick and easy way to find out what people are saying on Twitter, right now. It's so easy—just go to the engine, enter your search term (such as the name of your business or the name of your competitor's business) and see what you get.

> **2.2 Action Idea: Take 15 minutes today and visit one or two of the sites we discuss. See if any of them feel like a site you would feel comfortable visiting and using regularly. If you find one, then make that the key focus of your online listening. If not, visit one or two more tomorrow and keep sampling the sites until you find the ones that suit you.**

- If you currently have a Twitter account, try TweetBeep (http://www.tweetbeep.com) to keep track of what people are talking about on Twitter. It's similar to Google Alerts and Social Mention, but focuses only on Twitter. Sign up for an account and enter your Twitter name, and you will get updates on conversations about your business.

Good Conversations

The good conversations—the ones in which people say positive things about your business and recommend it to others—are great to hear because you know you're doing things right. You can see how your own decisions about running the business have positively influenced people's lives. Moreover, these conversations help you know what to promote about your business: for example, if you find out people really like a new brand of shampoo or a new flavor of ice cream that you sell, promote that in your other communications.

You can always reach out and connect with the people who are saying positive things about your business. If someone comments on their blog that they had a great interaction with your salesperson, leave a comment with a thank you. That goes a long way toward building a strong brand and assures people someone is listening to them. Adam Cuppy (Dutch Bros. Coffee) sees an additional benefit. He said "you might not be able to [thank people] all the time, but you have to praise them, because then they'll be more forgiving in the future if something does go wrong."

The Laughing Planet Café comments on every tweet and Facebook post that mentions the café. Additionally, the café tries to keep the conversations going by asking questions of the person who posts. If someone posts that their meal was delicious, for example, the café will thank them for the comment, then ask what they had to eat and at which location. That simple response started a conversation in which the customer named the specific location and mentioned the specific meal she was having. This is terrific word of mouth for the café. Similarly, if someone mentions a specific meal that they enjoyed, the café will thank them and then comment on some of the ingredients in the meal. That way, the original poster feels appreciated, and other people can learn a bit more about the business. All these types of tweets provide additional information to positive comment and encourage more conversations between the restaurant and customers and among customers themselves.

You can also use these good reviews in your other message tactics. For example, you might want to include quotes from positive reviews in your newsletter or other marketing messages. If you're on Twitter, you can use the "retweet" function to share a positive message from a customer with the rest of your network. Sometimes, too, your business might be mentioned in a neutral way. Someone might post "I met my friends across the street from the Main Street Diner." If that happens, then leave a comment, such as inviting them in to have a cup of coffee the next time they are in the neighborhood.

> 2.3 Action Idea: Trey Pitsenger (Golden Gekko) said it best: "You can give the customer an experience worth writing about, and that will be your best form of advertising: customers spreading the word, and other potential customers deciding whether to visit you or not based on the reviews."

When the Conversation Goes Bad

We all love it when a customer raves about our business. But what about when customers don't rave about our business and want to tell the world? Every business involved with social media will inevitably have some customer who posts a negative comment. That's just part of the digital environment. Yet many business owners are so frightened by this idea that they avoid social media altogether in fear that they will lose control of their brand. But if you constantly monitor messages online, you'll be the first to hear the bad news, and hopefully the first to respond to it. In the end, you will take *control* of the conversation when it might have otherwise been left to fester unaddressed.

Kelli Matthews (Café Yumm!) believes it is important to embrace the negative. Kelli told us, "it's really an opportunity for you to respond to your customer's questions and concerns and fears and problems in a way that's live and everyone else can see how you're dealing with it. And ultimately, I think, builds a lot of credibility and a lot of trust." This credibility is important for small businesses, and responding to customers should be an important part of your—and your staff's—job. Jesse Yu (Qoola) told us that every comment is important, because the customer had the type of experience that caused them to leave the business, go home, get on the computer, and talk about the experience. So regardless of whether the experience was good or bad, the customer spent time and energy posting the comment, and responding to the customer will show that you appreciate the effort your customer went through, whether the experience was positive or negative. Jesse discusses these types of comments with his team, and they decide how to proceed: whether to apologize, whether to explain a policy, and how the problem will be addressed. Then, they make sure the original poster gets a response describing the discussion.

This notion of getting the team involved is important. It is likely that you rely on your team of employees to help you run your business, and they need to take responsibility for both good and bad comments. The team can also help in monitoring the social web to hear all the messages that are out there. Adam Wallace (Roger Smith Hotel) thinks it is important that everyone on the team keep an eye out for what is happening in social media. According to Adam, employees need to understand the effects of customer conversations about their experiences, especially their negative experiences, which can be communicated via social media to hundreds of people.

Keep in mind, though, that whoever responds to the negative review should clearly understand your business mission and how social media fits into your goals. Adam Cuppy (Dutch Bros. Coffee) had an experience in which a response to a negative comment came off as too much like advertising and not enough like customer service. In Chapter 4, we'll share more about the importance of a consistent voice.

Negative reviews can be a positive opportunity for your business. The Roger Smith Hotel staff have had situations in which customers have used the hotel's Facebook page to complain about the company. One customer had tried to arrange a party on short notice, and the hotel determined they didn't have enough staff for the party and had no choice but to cancel it. In this case, the hotel deserved the "scathing rant" that the customer left on the Facebook page:

> [The customer said] she would never recommend us, what awful service, how could we do this. And we caught it, we wrote to her right back on our fan page, and responded with e-mail and a phone number, asking her to get in touch, and she wrote back to me, and we had about five e-mails back and forth in the course of the day. By the end of the day, she had not only booked the party, but invited Adam and I to be on one of her webinars this spring about how to use social media in customer service.

The customer eventually asked if she should remove her rant from the Facebook page. How did the hotel reply? They asked her not to delete it. They wanted customers to see how they dealt with negative comments. The customer then went back to the Facebook page and wrote another long post, this time a very positive one, focusing on how surprised she was that someone read her negative comment and responded to it, and eventually fixed the problem.

In this case, it was the ease of being able to post the negative comment that made the customer want to do it. Adam Wallace asked her if she would have called or written to the hotel directly, and the customer said she wouldn't—but she would have told all of her friends never to use the hotel. Without the negative Facebook comment, the hotel would never have been able to correct the situation and win a customer for life.

Utah Dave Robison (Salt Lake City Realtor) would certainly agree with these decisions made and refers to these actions in terms of transparency:

the idea that instead of covering up something bad that someone says about you, you try to go back and fix it. Dave thinks it's inevitable that someone is going to say something bad about your business and believes it is better to play offense, since there is no value in just playing defense. He contacts people via email, phone, or through social networks to try to resolve any problems that arise. According to Dave, "how you address the complaint is really what's important, rather than trying not to have them out there."

Lisa Hartwick (Hartwick's Kitchen Store) uses social media to address both positive and negative comments. When someone posts a positive statement on Twitter, for example, she tweets back her thanks and says that she'll pass the word to the rest of the team. She also tells the customer to let her know directly if she ever has a bad experience. She invites negative feedback. Lisa sees negative feedback as a way to learn what your business is doing wrong and how the business can improve.

Sometimes, unfortunately, negative reviews can be posted not by customers, but by competitors. Jesse Yu (Qoola) talked about what happened after he opened a new branch of his yogurt store in Vancouver, Canada. Right after the store opened, a number of negative reviews were posted at the website http://www.urbanspoon.com. Jesse spent a little time looking not only at the comments, but also at the names of the posters, and noticed that they were all new posters to Urbanspoon who hadn't posted reviews of any other establishment at the site. Jesse assumes, then, that these negative comments are from competitors trying to get negative publicity for the new store, and thinks of it as "part of the game."

The website Yelp.com, for example, allows customers to review different businesses, and it allows businesses to respond back. On Yelp, one person stated that Lisa Hartwick's store had "too much" in terms of the amount of merchandise: the customer felt overwhelmed in the store. Lisa felt that there isn't much she could do to respond to that, as that is how the individual personally felt. However, recommending to the poster that she simply ask for help might be a way to diffuse future criticisms of the store.

Patty Miller (Tattered Cover Bookstore) also prefers not to engage with negative reviews on sites like Yelp, but rather tries to send the individual a private response to learn more about the problem and address their bad feelings. Often Patty or someone on her staff sends the poster an incentive, such as a gift card, in order to entice the person back to the store. One time, however, Patty noticed a situation in which there was discussion among users on a customer review site about which bookstore was better, the Tattered Cover or Powell's Bookstore in Oregon. The conversation began to get heated, with posters taking sides; the tone began to become negative and antagonistic. At this point, Patty felt she had to weigh in and said, "You know, it really doesn't matter. Powell's is our friend, and we are for all of you who shop at Powell's. So there's really no debate here." In that way, Patty diffused a negative conversation and refocused the comments back to where she wanted them to be: popular books and good in-store experiences.

Keep in mind, too, that running a business is not a perfect science. Things go wrong, and many customers realize that a single incidence of a problem with a business is not necessarily indicative of how the business works on a daily basis. The important thing is how you handle problems; and again, without social media listening, you might not be able to know a problem exists. Jesse Yu (Qoola) told us, "We know that we can't maintain a stellar performance all the time, because we're still a growing business." He thinks that the fact that the owners are there, in the store, talking to customers, helps to overcome many operational problems. Lisa Hartwick (Hartwick's Kitchen Store) agrees. "Everyone knows that things go wrong," said Lisa. "There's no perfect science. It's just like you can go eat at your favorite restaurant and one night it's just awful you're so disappointed. Chances are you're probably going to give them another try and it may be great again. So I think most people understand that."

The bad conversations are hard to hear, but they are important to hear, too. Learn from these bad reviews. The worst thing to do is to ignore them. See if there are aspects of your business you need to change. If an employee was rude, or service was slow, or a product did not perform as anticipated, you have the opportunity, at a minimum, to apologize to the person (by leaving a comment on their blog or Facebook page, or wherever the bad comment occurred). You can also tell them that you plan to fix the problem (and how), and perhaps offer them an incentive to come back to your business and try again. You can use information to make your business better.

The personal nature of a small business is valuable, and the value of sites like Yelp.com is that customers can scan many reviews and get an idea of the general tone of the reviews: whether they are predominantly good or predominantly bad. So don't be afraid of negative feedback. Take time to fix the problem, and then let people know the problem was fixed.

Be sure to tell your customers about the changes that you make based on customer response. You can use your own social media, and you can also promote this in your business. Celebrate the fact that you learned from your mistakes and are making positive changes to the company. Some businesses invite people to visit again or to re-review the site. The Bleeding Heart Bakery in Chicago went through a period in which they received a number of poor reviews, and they changed a lot of their process in order to address the problems. Then they developed a promotion that gave a free cupcake to anyone who brought in a bad review that they had previously posted on Yelp. This was very successful in reintroducing people to the bakery.

> **2.4 Action Idea:** It only takes a few seconds to thank someone for a positive review. Addressing negative reviews will take a bit more time. Find the time to respond to every negative review.

When an Unhappy Person Keeps Complaining

One big challenge that many businesses face is the person who won't stop: who says negative things about your business and who will not stop saying them even after you've apologized profusely, fixed the problem, and offered them a discount or a rebate to address their issue. Frankly, there are people who never want to back down. Southwest Airlines had to face this recently when movie director Kevin Smith had a bad experience on a Southwest flight. Smith, a somewhat large man, was ejected from a Southwest Airlines flight because the captain believed his excessive weight posed a safety risk. Basically, the seat was too small to accommodate his girth, and there were concerns he couldn't wear a safety belt. Southwest has a specific policy for dealing with large people—they ask them to buy two seats. Within minutes, Kevin Smith started tweeting about this experience. At first, the tweets were benign (Smith tweeted, "I know I'm fat, but was Captain Leysath really justified in throwing me off a flight for which I was already seated?") but as the day wore on, Smith's anger with the airline escalated, and his tweets became profanity-filled diatribes against Southwest. Smith tweeted more than 20 anti-Southwest tweets over the course of about three hours (including an hour of flight time).

Southwest did respond, and did so in a timely manner: customer service representatives called him at the number listed on his ticket (which was a home phone number, and not a cell phone; thus Smith did not get the messages during his tweak-out) and the Southwest people also tweeted that Smith had a phone message waiting for him. These are all good tactics, and would appease most people.

However, Smith is not most people. He tweeted that the only reason that Southwest called him was because he "has a platform to express his displeasure." Since the tweak-out occurred, Southwest has been chastised for choosing to eject an arguably "famous" person who has almost two million followers on Twitter. Our point of view is that everyone has a platform to express their displeasure. It's called word of mouth, and companies need to be aware that people are using these platforms regularly. Tracking and addressing the complaints, like Southwest did, is an appropriate response. Attacking Southwest for not being able to recognize "celebrities" like Kevin Smith, and treat them differently from other passengers, like many other tweeters did, is not fair.

And you know what? People on Twitter recognized this. After the initial round of anti-Southwest tweets, people started telling Smith to back off. The tweets were along the lines of "Give it a rest, I understand @Southwest was bad to you." Eventually, Smith stopped.

The lesson here is that yes, you must address the negative comments about your business. When it escalates, like it did in this case, the best thing to do is repeat what you've said and done already. Don't try to argue with someone who is "off the rails"—you know you won't win, and you risk lowering yourself to their level. Also, keep in mind that others likely will jump in to support and defend you, or at a minimum to tell the individual that he or she has made their point and is acting like a jerk.

Southwest addressed this situation later on their blog. Some new information about the incident was provided: that Smith was originally booked on a different flight where he had reserved two seats, but changed plans to get an earlier flight where two seats were not available. He received a $100 voucher in response to his distress. The company reiterated their safety policy that allows captains to remove individuals who appear to

be safety risks. Also, the blog post mentioned Smith was a regular flier (and booker of two seats) on the airline: information that probably was over the top to provide, but does make the point.

While this was a frustrating and embarrassing time for Southwest, they did everything right. They treated Smith like they would treat any other customer, with the exception of probably responding more publicly to his "tweak-out" than they would to say, me, if I complained. They had a policy, and they stuck to it. They responded as quickly as they possibly could, and they didn't get angry or defensive in their tweets. They let the community join in to try to calm Smith down, which worked. These are great lessons for dealing with negative word of mouth.

When Nobody Talks

What happens when a few days go by, and you learn that no one is talking about your business? This is the time to encourage your customers to talk about your business at review sites. Sometimes all people need is to be asked. Brad Niva (Rogue Wilderness Adventures) sends follow-up emails to clients after their rafting or hiking trips and invites them to add a review on either Yelp.com or Insider Pages. He believes that "at least 98% of customers had a good experience" and so feels very comfortable making this request. Robbie Vitrano (Naked Pizza) does this all the time. The Naked Pizza staffers ask the customers they meet in the store to go to Yelp.com and give them a review. Also, if they find people that are tweeting about their pizzas or posting positive comments on Facebook, they'll leave a comment or a tweet asking them to go to Yelp or Urbanspoon and mention the brand there. Robbie says that when he is giving interviews to the press and talking about his brand, he finds that "a lot of times they'll go to Yelp and want to see [what people are actually saying], it's kind of a validation of my opinion."

At the Roger Smith Hotel, the front desk agents are in charge of promoting the review sites to customers when they check out. The agents at the desk say something to the effect of "we hope you enjoyed your stay, and if you'd let us know what you thought on TripAdvisor." If a guest connects with the hotel via social media after their stay, the hotel will often politely ask they post a review of their trip on TripAdvisor or Yelp.

Social media is a huge megaphone for word of mouth. Before social media, people passed on recommendations and complaints in face-to-face conversations, one on one, but now one person can influence the perception of your business among hundreds or even thousands of people. The bottom line is, people love to talk. Some will talk without your encouragement, and others will not, but a little bit of encouragement goes a long way. The important thing to remember is once they start talking, you need to listen and respond.

Key Chapter Insights

- Listening to conversations will help you know what people are saying about you so you can address their problems and think about messages to promote your business. You can only start using social media if you have first listened to what's being said.

- Listening first gives you the edge in social content and differentiation from competitors.

- Evaluate monitoring sites and select the one(s) that have the greatest impact on your category of business.

- Thank the advocates of your business: you will create more in the process.

- Always respond to negative comments, and some will become advocates.

- You can never outtalk a continually negative person. Stand by what you have done. The rest of the audience will respect you.

Getting Started

- If you are brand new to social media: Visit Yelp.com and register for an account so you can track what your customers are saying. Set up a "Google alert" for your business and one on SocialMention.com as well.

- If you are familiar with social media: Develop a "listening" strategy that will have you visiting these review sites regularly. Start to keep track of positive comments that you can use in future messages, and begin to respond to any types of negative messages you see.

- If you are ready to move to the next level: Start listening to what people are saying about your competitors. This can help you exploit a weakness in your competition's marketing strategy.

Getting Started with Blogging

If you've been on the Internet in the last few years, you've probably heard the term "blog." Blogs are all over the web now and cover just about any subject you can think of. In January 2010, there were an estimated 126 million blogs available online.

"Blog" is shorthand for "weblog," which is defined as a website in the form of an ongoing journal. Blogs chronicle information, and they are expected to be updated regularly. Unlike Facebook or Twitter, blogs typically cover subjects in greater depth and detail.

Most blogs have a theme. Some you may have heard of are Mashable, a social media blog, or Huffington Post, a news and commentary blog. The best blogs are written by people who are knowledgeable about the subject matter, but you don't need to look very hard to find a great many blogs that aren't. That's because blogs are an easy online publishing platform to establish, and there are more than a few sites like WordPress and Blogger that can have you blogging in a matter of minutes. These online services even let you customize the blog's appearance, add pages with additional information, and link your blog to other social media sites. If you don't have a website, a blog, in conjunction with a Facebook and/or Twitter account, can be a good substitute.

Choosing a Style

Blogs take on different shapes and sizes, and it is helpful to note the different types out there so you know what's available to you when you want to begin your own blog, whether for yourself or your company.

Personal Blogs

- What they are: Personal blogs are essentially online diaries. They are almost always written by a single author who writes about his or her life on a regular basis.
- What they are good for: Blogs allow for sharing details of one's personal life. Unless the writer has an exceptionally interesting life or a wild imagination, these can be boring, but celebrities and prominent businesspeople have built huge online followings with blogs like these.
- Who writes them:
  - Prominent individuals within a community

- ○   Creative writers
- ○   People with (interesting) daily experiences germane to an industry or field
- Examples of personal blogs:
    - ○   Earth to Holly blog (http://earthtoholly.com/)
    - ○   Zappos CEO and COO blog (http://blogs.zappos.com/blogs/ceo -and-coo-blog)

Corporate Blogs

- What they are: Corporate blogs are written on behalf of a company by one or more writers. Most often, corporate blogs deal with the company itself and any new developments. They can also be a platform for press releases. They are often cited as the "official" blog and can be referenced by outside organizations as being the official opinion of the company.
- What they are good for:
    - ○   Larger companies needing a single voice
    - ○   Companies with a steady stream of new developments that would be interesting to a larger community
    - ○   Companies looking to establish a more formal online identity than what's possible with Facebook or Twitter
- Who writes them
    - ○   The author may not be named, but noted as the company itself
    - ○   The CEO
    - ○   The PR firm for the company, yet signed by the CEO
- Examples:
    - ○   Official Google Blog (http://googleblog.blogspot.com/)
    - ○   The Official Palm Blog (http://blog.palm.com)

Genre Blogs

- What they are: Genre blogs focus on a niche. If done well, they are a valuable resource to others interested in that niche. A good genre blog can define individuals as experts in their field and innovators or, if nothing else, a helpful and interested online voice.

- What they are good for:
  - People with a deep expertise in a certain area
  - Business owners looking to establish industry credibility
  - Companies that want to add value and currency to their website with in-depth information.
- Who writes them: Individuals who are knowledgeable about a specific topic.
- Examples:
  - Freakonomics: (http://freakonomics.blogs.nytimes.com)
  - Mashable
  - Treehugger

Microblogs

- What they are: Microblogs are short, "mini" blogs. Twitter is considered a microblog, as is Tumblr, a website designed for posting lots of media-like photos and videos quickly in blog style, so each new post appears on top of the older one. Microblogs don't require the attention a full blog post would, which means they are more likely to be read completely. See Chapter 4a for more information.

Choosing a Site to Host Your Blog

Several free sites will host your blog. These sites work somewhat similarly and offer different capabilites. A comparison is found in Table 2a.1.

Because of its offering and flexibility, we recommend starting with a WordPress blog.

Creating a WordPress Blog

1. Visit http://www.wordpress.com.
2. Click on the link, "Sign up now."
3. Enter your personal information.
4. Choose the name and title of your blog. Choose a title that describes something about the blog itself. The URL name should be the title, or if it's too long, perhaps

TABLE 2A.1
Blogging Choices

	WordPress	Blogger	Moveable Type
Cost?	Free	Free	Free Plus, depending on usage
Multiple authors	Yes	Yes	Yes
Blogroll (list of favorite blogs appearing on sidebar)?	Yes	No	Yes
Can you get traffic stats?	Yes, via plugin	Yes, via third-party software (Google Analytics)	Yes, via plugin
Can you divide posts into categories?	Yes	No	Yes

an abbreviated version or just your name. Unless you plan to post sensitive information, we recommend leaving the privacy box checked so your blog can be easily found.

5. Go to your email inbox and click on the WordPress confirmation link. You will be taken to your blog.

6. Go back to the WordPress.com site and log in with your username and password.

7. Click on the "My Dashboard" tab.

8. It is from this dashboard that you will administer your entire blog. From here, you can write news posts, approve comments, change the appearance of your blog, and view your blog viewership stats, among other things. WordPress has many useful tools and plugins that can be utilized once you become more familiar with the interface, but for now, we'll just cover the basics.

Writing a New Post

Writing posts are the essence of blogs and should be your first priority. Below are instructions to get started:

1. From the main dashboard, click on "Posts." Check the "Hello World" entry and delete it. It's a sample filler post to show you how your blog posts will look.

2. From the Posts page, you will be able to see a list of your posts. Right now, this section will be empty.

3. From the menu beneath "Posts," click on "Add new."

4. Enter your title and start blogging.

5. Remember to save your draft regularly. When you're finished, click "Preview." If you're happy with the way everything looks, click "Publish," and you're done!

6. You have the option of editing old posts if you want to add or remove anything. From the list of Posts, hover over the title of the relevant post and click "Edit."

Adding Pictures or Movies

Inserting images and videos is a snap; all you need to have is the file on your computer.

1. There are several icons next to the "Upload/Insert" text just above the field where you write your blog.

2. Hover your cursor over each and select the option relevant to your needs.

3. For pictures, for instance, you can select your file, and WordPress will do the rest. There are a few more options you can easily customize, such as the alignment of the photo and how big it appears.

Organizing Posts with Categories

Adding categories is a way to classify your posts according to subgenres. A cooking blog might have categories like meat, vegetables, soups, desserts, breads, etc. Categories allow your readers to view all your posts that are relevant to their subinterests within your blog.

1. From the dashboard, click on "Posts."

2. From the drop-down menu, click on "Categories."

3. Add as many new categories as you like, although we recommend keeping this number to 4–6, unless you plan on writing on an expansive list of topics.

4. Once you have added your new categories, deleted the "uncategorized" category, as it is now unnecessary.

5. When you write a new post, remember to categorize your post using the toolbar on the right- hand side entitled, "Categories." You can do this for old posts, too.

Customizing the Appearance of Your Blog

To make your blog stand out, you will want something different from the default that will help differentiate your blog from others. Here, we'll show you how to make some basic adjustments to the blog's layout.

Picking a Theme

1. From your dashboard, click on the "Appearance" tab on the lower left-hand side.

2. Click on "Themes."

3. Here you can select from a wide variety of different themes, each of which will give your blog a different vibe. To preview how your blog will look with the new theme, just click "Preview." If you're happy with the new theme, click "Activate," and it will become your own. Remember, the goal of a blog is first and foremost to be functional, so picking a clean, simple theme is always a good choice.

Customizing Information

It's easy to customize what information appears on the right side of your blog, next to your posts. You can choose to show your latest posts, an archive of past posts, a calendar, information about yourself, etc.

1. From the main dashboard, click on the "Appearance" tab on the lower left-hand side.

2. Click on "Widgets."

3. From here, you can drag and drop "Widgets" into the right column, also called a sidebar.

4. The most popular choices are, in this order: search, recent posts, archives, and categories. We recommend including the text widget after search, where you can write a little about yourself as an author.

5. Play around a bit. When you want to see how your changes are reflected on your blog, just click on your blog's name on the upper right-hand corner.

There are a number of other appearance-related options that you can use to customize your blog. You'll be able to learn most of these options easily, but if you have trouble, you can always find answers in the WordPress support section.

Tips for Successful Blogging

- Have a consistent presence: most successful bloggers post a new entry at least every other day.

- Vary the content of your blogs. Review the messaging recommendations in Chapter 4 to get some great ideas on different types of content you can use.

- Limit self-promotion. Direct self-promotion rarely works. Use the "Categories" feature to make sure you are not dedicating the majority of your blog to a single topic.

- Track and measure your activities on Twitter: see Chapter 7 for information.

3

Building Relationships: How to Build Social Networks and Engage Customers Using Social Media

> We just recently integrated our YouTube channel onto our Facebook fan page, we integrated our Flickr page onto our Facebook fan page. We integrate our blog on there, so I think they're really trying to make Facebook sort of a one stop shop for being everything about business, and that says that Facebook is hugely powerful.
>
> —Adam Wallace (Roger Smith Hotel)

Why do most small businesses start using social media? Generally, for the wrong reasons. Most small businesses want to have a social media presence simply because the social media site provides a free space for the business to stake a claim. We refer to these businesses as taking the "field of dreams" approach to using social media. Small businesses think, "If I build it, they will come." Occasionally, this works: very strong brands that already have communities of users—people who are highly loyal to their brand—are primed to find a community of users in the social media space right away. Most retailers, however, will have to put some effort into creating a dynamic media presence. By dynamic, we mean a space with engaged, active participants, not merely a one-way promotional channel for a business. The key to all of this is spending time to build relationships with individuals in the social media space.

Additionally, a goal for small businesses using social media is not only to engage with the people visiting the site, but also to encourage the visitors to interact with each other. This interaction is important because it creates content that should interest other customers, it creates word of mouth in both traditional and digital media, it allows you to spend more time listening and less time creating content, and, most importantly, it signals you have a brand worth caring about.

In this chapter, we will discuss how businesses decide where they should build their social networks, and discuss ways to create a sense of community on your site.

Find Your Nerve Center

You are busy. You have a business to run, a family to connect with, and probably some charity or community obligations on top of that. Now you might be thinking about adding online participation in social networks, too! Where do you begin? The first step is to figure out where you want to be. Dozens of social media sites are available for you to be a part of, and it's tempting to be a part of everything. Instead, try to focus on the social media sites that best fit your brand rather than spreading yourself too thin across all of them. Even though the upfront costs of social media are zero, they require a tremendous amount of time and diligence to do well.

Many businesses start with what Jesse Yu (Qoola) calls "the triumvirate of social media . . . Twitter, Facebook, and MySpace." However, the popularity of MySpace is in steep decline, especially among post adolescent users, and more businesses are migrating to a third leg of the social media stool using a text site like a blog, a photographic site like Flickr, or a video site like YouTube. Businesses are also investigating the next generation of social media, including mobile (think iPhone apps) and geolocation with services like Foursquare. Jesse says the no-cost nature of social media makes it tempting to want to be involved everywhere, especially when you know your customers are involved in all different types of social media.

How do you decide which to use? You could take Jesse Yu's (Qoola) approach: he wants to be where their customers are, when their customers are online. That ubiquitous strategy works for Qoola, which is a small, growing business owned by young, energetic individuals who were already digitally savvy. However, it may not work for your business if you are not as familiar with social media as Jesse and his team. As a first step, then, you should take some time and explore what your competitors are doing online (see Chapter 8 for a complete description of the social audit). Examine both your national and your local competitors, and see what social media they are using and what review sites tend to cover their business. Once you find where your competition is in the social sphere, try to gauge where they are spending most of their online time. Where do they post most frequently; where do they interact? This is one way to help you determine the best places for you to start.

Building an online community and nurturing it for your business's success takes time, and your day is filled with various demands that also need attention. Therefore, for many businesses, the best thing to do will be to start out by limiting your participation in social networks to a few, say one to three, at first. How do you decide where?

First, think about which social media you currently use regularly: either personally, or for your business. Starting with optimizing the social media platforms you are already on will serve you better than spreading yourself thin for the sake of being everywhere online.

Next, find out what social media your customers use. A general rule of thumb online is go to where your customers are; don't make them come to you. Find out where your customers are by conducting informal polls at the register, or send out a poll or inquiry via your regular newsletter. After you find out where your customers are, ask how they're using it (for business use, for personal use, for shopping, to keep up with family and friends, etc.), and whether they would be interested in being part of your business's community at that social media site. Target the places where you have the best chance of building an active community.

For example, you may find that either all your customers tend to be primarily on Facebook, or that all your customers avoid social media and prefer reading blogs. If that is the case, then you know where you should be! But in most cases, it is likely that some of your customers will prefer Facebook, some will prefer Twitter, and some will prefer something else altogether. This indicates you will likely need some type of presence in different places.

However, you should probably decide that one of the social media sites is going to be your "nerve center," the place in which you are going to put most of your effort and your time. Robbie Vitrano (Naked Pizza) sees the value in the nerve center idea: "[the social media you choose] becomes more successful because it's the one that you use and the one you like to use." It also helps you set the priorities for where you spend your time online: you start with the nerve center first and, if time allows, focus on your secondary social media presences. Also, many sites allow "cross posting," where a post at one site like Twitter will also show up on Facebook. This synchronization allows you to be in several places at once. Keep in mind, though, that Facebook and Twitter are different types of sites that customers use for different reasons, so "cross posting," while convenient, doesn't always yield the best results.

Another consideration in selecting your nerve center is how often and how quickly you are going to be able to respond to people. With Twitter, there is an expectation among people there that you will respond quickly to conversations. With Facebook and blogs, a rapid response is not always necessary.

If you have a nerve center, you will also feel more dedicated and connected since you will be able to see results as you work on building the community. How should you select your nerve center? Robbie Vitrano (Naked Pizza) explains that the one social media site that resonates with you the most is the best choice for our nerve center. Therefore, when you find the social media tool that is right for you, the one you feel comfortable with, consider that as your nerve center.

Facebook as Nerve Center

Many companies, including Naked Pizza, have selected Facebook for their nerve center. Of all the social media sites, Facebook has the most complete framework for a host of different activities, meaning you can post photos, videos, updates, and details about your business; create discussions; and even advertise your page. Some big companies have even decided to use their Facebook pages as their websites, because that is where their customers are. Typically, Facebook is a more personal environment. Facebook tends to accommodate closer relationships and longer conversations among users. This is perfect if you have a business, product, or service that people feel strongly about or feel that they are connected to personally.

Robbie Vitrano (Naked Pizza) considers Facebook their nerve center because, from a penetration standpoint, Facebook reaches the most customers. Additionally, people at Naked Pizza like Facebook and are very familiar with it. The range of applications and tools make it easy for Naked Pizza to keep it, in Robbie's words, "fluid and flowing and engaging with people on a regular basis." Jesse Yu (Qoola) also likes Facebook because it offers a semblance of a threaded discussion, similar to an online discussion board, where customers can talk about the restaurant, like what their favorite flavors are. He also believes he has more control over messages with a Facebook page. He can easily ask questions about flavors, or even ask fans how they feel about certain flavors, or quickly see both the positive and negative responses, and the entire discussion, or thread, is visible to everyone.

JP Poloway (Mountain Trek) and Daniel Pollard (Pelican Brew Pub and Restaurant) both see Facebook as important for their types of businesses, which are destination-oriented. Mountain Trek, a weeklong hiking boot camp program in Canada, uses Facebook to share images of adventures and to allow potential customers to get a good idea of what their adventure week would be like. Facebook also points clients to the website for more information. Daniel promotes weekend events at the pub during the week in order to attract weekend visitors to the Oregon coast to stop by the pub. Both businesses also think Facebook is a great place for customers to relive their experiences once they are back to their normal lives.

This measurement aspect, and the ease of tracking users and their responses, is also appealing to Brian Mason (SKP-Popcorn). He uses the business's Facebook page specifically to get information about interest and attendance at fund-raising events. Similarly, Adam Cuppy (Dutch Bros. Coffee) found Facebook as an easy way to get an online presence, and found that many of his customers seek out the business's Facebook page. He also likes Facebook as a customer service tool because customers can follow the interactions between a poster and the business; following such a conversation on Twitter can be difficult if one user doesn't follower both parties in a conversation.

Utah Dave Robison (Realtor) considers Facebook a great source for leads. He finds that the majority of his Facebook friends are first-time homebuyers, and Facebook allows enough space to provide information— such as home listings—as well as tools like private messaging that allow for one-on-one communication with potential clients. In this way, Facebook becomes a one-stop shop for multiple communication needs.

Patty Miller (Tattered Cover Bookstore) finds that people on Facebook are the people she sees most often in the store. Since so many of her Facebook fans are local, Facebook is a perfect way to announce events. The staff at the bookstore also direct Facebook fans to the website, where products can be purchased online.

Twitter as Nerve Center

Twitter is real-time social media at its best, but it requires constant updating and involvement. Because anyone can follow anyone, and mentioning someone is as easy as typing the "@" sign before their username, Twitter can be a great place for constant, informal conversations and sharing. For businesses that have constant updates they'd like to share with their community, or promotions that they hope will go viral, Twitter is a terrific resource.

Many businesses prefer Twitter as their nerve center for its simplicity alone. William Kennedy (CD World) enjoys discussing new records and music industry news with his customers on Twitter. He believes that Facebook can often feel "too personal" for business. Twitter also allows a business to deliver communications about products and services more quickly than Facebook. As William describes it, sending a sales message for CD World via Twitter seems more authentic and appropriate than the same message on Facebook. Because the business's followers can easily retweet messages (meaning messages can be forwarded by *your* followers to *your followers'* followers), tweets can spread quickly among online users.

Adam Wallace (Roger Smith Hotel) believes Twitter works well in reaching out and attracting new people into the network quickly because of the timely nature of the medium. Tweets are short, and people tend to send them frequently. Therefore, there are many more opportunities for someone to find your messages on Twitter and to decide to follow you or forward your message to their followers.

Twitter is not for everyone, though. Jesse Yu (Qoola) finds Twitter harder to use to establish a community. Since so many conversations are already happening, it is difficult and challenging to "jump into the fray." Jesse and JP Poloway (Mountain Trek) also expressed concerns about the high level of competition and clutter on Twitter. Jesse was concerned that people are not hearing everything that Qoola tweets because of the clutter, and that some people follow hundreds or thousands of different people on Twitter. As such, Twitter might work better for businesses that have already established a strong online community.

Blog as Nerve Center

Many individuals and businesses have blogs. If you like to write and have a lot of important information to share with others, a blog is a great outlet for you. Troy Pitsenger (Golden Gecko Garden Store) is known as the Blogging Nurseryman, and he believes much of his business success is due to his blog. Trey says:

> Because of the blog my nursery, which is really a small mom and pop operation, is known by more people than would otherwise know about it. We also show up in lots of searches. We have great search engine optimization. I also blog to just write my thoughts. It helps people to know the owner of the garden center better. It's just an ongoing conversation I am having with whomever wants to listen and comment.

3.1 Action Idea: Want to be known as an industry expert? It is as simple as setting up Google Alerts (visit http://www.google.com/alerts for complete instructions on how to set up your own alerts). Enter search terms that apply to both your business and to the topics your customers are interested in. For example, Richie Vintrano (Naked Pizza) has Google Alerts set up for technology, design, science, and food, based on aspects of their product. He also includes nutrition and cultural information in his Google Alerts, because he knows his target is interested in those areas.

Remember, each time you post on your blog, Google will index it and will potentially direct relevant searches to your page in the search results (see Chapter 5 for more information on optimizing your sites for search engines).

Jillian Bisinger and Tony Zucca (Julian Bisinger Modern Photography) started their social media activity with their blog and now see it as central to their social media presence. They use their blog to post a photo or two from recent shoots: these photos give customers a "teaser" of what their actual photos will look like, and customers comment on the photos and share them with others. Recently, though, business has been so good that only a select number of photos are shared on the blog. This gets clients talking and wondering whether their photos will be "blogworthy"—and that starts a lot of positive word of mouth for the business.

Robbie Vitrano (Naked Pizza) values the ability to connect the store's blog with other media they use. Robbie uses Twitter to link tweets to the blog, as well as to "tease" information about the blog. Since the staff at Naked Pizza tweet frequently, the tweets that they've done remind them to write more blog posts so that they can tweet about them. If you are present on multiple sites, making sure you have links to those sites can create synergy across your social media profile, so people who read you blog can easily connect with you on Facebook, or if they follow you on Twitter, can easily jump to your blog.

Utah Dave Robison (Realtor) also sees the connections. Utah Dave believes his blog serves a specific audience. He describes it this way:

> The blog usually targets people that are interested in buying a home and they're interested in learning. I call them researchers. And their personality is they're usually slower to make a commitment or slower to make decision. But they'll read everything they can about the real estate, about the market, about you. And as they do that, they'll become familiar with you and they think they know you. And then, they will come to you, and then they're more comfortable.

Adam Wallace (Roger Smith Hotel) is a big supporter of blogs for all these reasons. He said:

> A blog provides a place where you can be engaging and interacting with people and having people interact with your brand on a daily basis . . . all of our YouTube videos are embedded on our blog, stories and photos and everything like that. You have to have a blog, then you still need content for the blog . . . we use Twitter and Facebook as distribution mechanisms and audience for the blog. I don't think you can cut corners here, and I don't think that you want to, because it's your online brand.

3.2 Action Idea: How do you easily integrate your Facebook and Twitter posts? One way is an application like TweetDeck (http://www.tweetdeck.com): You download this application onto your desktop, enter your login and password for both Facebook and Twitter, and you can select which messages get posted at both places. Alternatively, open both your Twitter and Facebook accounts using your web browser. Then, visit http://apps.facebook.com/twitter/ and follow the instructions to simultaneously post on both sites. You can also use an RSS feed to connect your blog to Facebook and Twitter; the website http://www.blogtotweet.com provides instructions.

Maximize Social Media's Potential

The ability to have different social network sites integrated among each other is incredibly valuable for a small business, both in terms of impact and in terms of time management.

The growth of social media means that many of the applications now interact with each other seamlessly. As we mentioned earlier, it is possible to cross-post something on Facebook and have it show up on Twitter, and vice versa. William Kennedy (CD World) enjoys being able to link his tweets directly to his Facebook wall, accomplishing his goal of "killing two birds with one stone." He sees Twitter as distributing information or interesting links, and Facebook as allowing for discussion and conversations about the information. Additionally, the cross-posting may allow businesses to reach two completely different audiences. Realtor Utah Dave Robison has witnessed minimal crossover in audiences among the social network sites. He finds that Facebook fans rarely read his blog, and so having one message go out to different audiences is a great time saver.

Businesses can also integrate photographic content from Flickr and video content from YouTube into their other social media. Adam Wallace (Roger Smith Hotel) integrates both Flickr and YouTube into Facebook, along with the blog. He sees Facebook as becoming less of a social media site and more of a portal, and wants to use that power to reach their customers and potential customers. Facebook has a terrific interface for integrating media of all sorts. Videos and pictures are great conversation starters and add some variety beyond text updates.

Creating a Community

Once you've determined which social networks you are going to focus on, the next step is to let people know you have established a presence on the specific social network site. Before you do anything else, you should make sure that your business website links to your social media sites. Alternatively, your website can feature a signup for emails or text messages, and this channel can be used to invite people to your social media sites. Paco Miller (Tia Juana's) has an email signup link that automatically generates an email adding the web visitor to the "guest list" for the Tia Juana nightclub that night. Once at the nightclub, more information can be collected about the guest. You can also include the links in your email newsletters, and perhaps even paint them on the side of your delivery vans. This simple step is often overlooked

Hartwick's Kitchen Store has a computer at a sales desk where in-store customers can sign up for Twitter or Facebook while they are waiting for a salesperson to run their charge or wrap their purchases. The store has also recruited people to their social network sites by handing out flyers in the store inviting customers to follow them on Facebook and Twitter. Paco Miller (Tia Juana's) collects contact information from customers via comment cards at the restaurant table. All the outlets of Dutch Bros. Coffee have point-of-purchase signage inviting customers to follow them on their social media sites. Adam Cuppy (Dutch Bros. Coffee) underscores the importance of an easy-to-remember site address so customers can easily find them and follow them. He stresses the importance of registering for a "vanity" profile name: for Dutch Bros. Coffee, the main Facebook page's URL is http://www.facebook .com/dutchbros and not a string of letters and numbers that are hard to remember.

> 3.3. Action Idea: Create an easy-to-remember name on Facebook here: http://www .facebook.com/username/.

Erica Leaf (Imagine Graphics) uses several tactics to generate traffic to social media. Recently, Imagine Graphics redesigned their website to add the Twitter and Facebook links prominently on the first page. Imagine Graphics also promotes their social media presence via their email newsletter, which is sent out every two to three weeks to a broad customer list. Erica believes consistent promotion of social media presence is key, especially if customers are not comfortable or familiar with social media. The more they see information about different social media, the higher the possibility that they will start to feel comfortable with the idea of social media, and the more likely they will decide to join.

Jesse Yu (Qoola) describes the process as being proactive and organic, since customers integrate social media into their lives, so requests to have customers participate in a business's social media must be organic as well. The Qoola stores feature signup sheets at the counter that allow patrons to provide their own information so Qoola can connect with them, not wait for the customer to connect with Qoola. The store's website features an electronic form where customers can provide their name, their Twitter and Facebook usernames, and their email. Jesse then reaches out individually to people who provide the information. He sees this as the start of the engagement process, which can help create a stronger community online.

Making the effort to personally invite people is a great tactic. Kelli Matthews (Cafe Yumm!) has a large personal network of friends and family. When Café Yumm! started their social media presence, she alerted her own personal networks on Facebook and Twitter of Cafe Yumm's new presence. As a result, people flocked to the site early and now Café Yumm! has over 1,000 followers on both Facebook and Twitter. Utah Dave Robison (Realtor) used a similar tactic. He emailed a link to all of his past and present customers inviting them to join his Facebook page, and he found that the vast majority of customers did so. At Dutch Bros. Coffee outlets, staff are instructed to invite people to follow them on social media if the topic of social media comes up during the course of the interaction between the barista and the customer. As previously mentioned, Paco Miller (Tia Juana's) has staff at the door of his nightclubs collecting phone numbers for texting purposes. He combines this information into a database, which can direct people to the social media sites as well as provide them with special offers.

When people sign up for your Facebook page, a notification will appear on their "news feed," a running list of notifications, which will also appear on the news feeds of that particular person's Facebook friends. This spreads the word about your page to the friends and family of the people who signed up for your page, and most businesspeople found that these notifications generated even more friends and fans for their pages. Somer

Deck (Fifth Street Public Market) experienced this firsthand. She told us that she first sent out the information about the blog and the Facebook site to all of her personal friends, as did other people who work for the small mall. That simple act started an avalanche of people joining the site.

Offering an incentive is also a great tactic to convince people to follow you, and incentives are great ways to develop word of mouth. Utah Dave Robison (Realtor) gave away an iPod to one lucky person who joined his site, and he promoted this contest in his emails. Lisa Hartwick (Hartwick's Kitchen Store) regularly gives away gift cards to followers on Facebook and Twitter. Once a month, she'll randomly select one Twitter follower and one Facebook follower, who each win a gift card to the store. This is promoted on the Facebook page and Twitter feed, and more often than not, the lucky winner also posts about it, which begins the word of mouth cycle anew.

Finally, it is possible to purchase advertisements on social media sites that can direct people to your page. Adam Cuppy (Dutch Bros. Coffee) reports that the greatest weekly increases in followers came during weeks when the company ran a small paid advertisement campaign on Facebook. Facebook advertising can be beneficial because it can be highly targeted. The Facebook website can give you much more information on taking advantage of this tactic.

> 3.4 Action Idea: Advertising on Facebook can help direct people to both your Facebook page and your store site. Facebook works on a "bidding" system in which you bid a certain amount for either impressions or click-throughs. More information is at http://www.facebook.com/advertising.

Have a Visible Presence

Once you have people at your site, the next step is to encourage them to engage with your site. One way to do this is for them to know that there is a real person—you or someone on your staff—actively monitoring and participating at the site. People come to social media to be social. Tony Zucca (Jillian Bisinger Modern Photography) has an interesting take on social media for small businesses. He believes that half of the reasons why people select a business is due the people involved in the business, and the value of social media is that it allows small businesses to create a feel for who customers will be working with: stories that can be told through words, images, and video. Tony also believes that once customers get a feel for the people who own and run the company, they recognize the value in the personal touch and will pay more for a small business's products than they would at a place like Wal-Mart or Target.

Customers not only need to know that this person exists, but also there is someone who is listening to them and who will respond to and engage with them. At some point, the people in your network are likely to visit you in person, and you can transfer a strong online relationship to the "real world." Adam Wallace (Roger Smith Hotel) described it this way:

> Our online presence is very active, very engaging, very of the moment, and we definitely try to pull that in when we see people specifically, who have reached out to us via any of our social channels, especially Twitter, or Facebook, or our blog. We make sure we meet them here in person, whether it is in the lobby for breakfast, or at one of the events they may be hosting. This is different from other hotels, where they bring people in through social media channels, but once you book your room, that's it. You know, at five o'clock, the employees leave their desk, and they go home. That's when our job sort of just gets beginning, that's when we really make that connection to the people.

Engaging your friends and fans starts with deciding how to present yourself with both words and images. Mark Beauchamp (Café Yumm!) talked to other businesspeople about social media and found many were using their faces, not their business logos, on their social media sites. Mark uses the logo for Café Yumm!'s business messages, but he also has a persona; an account where he is known as "YummGuy" and connects himself as the face behind the brand. He tries to be sure that everyone who follows the "business" page also follows his "personal" pages so they receive both the business messages and the "face behind the brand" messages. By having his personal account, he can mention personal things that are interesting but not necessarily directly relevant to Café Yumm! He finds this important since "you don't want to be necessarily talking about your kid's birthday party to your grocery store or restaurant customers.

They want to know that you're a real person, but they don't need to know what you personally are doing all of that time. So that balance is there."

Like most social media tactics, there is rarely a wrong way or a right way to do this. Erica Leaf (Imagine Graphics) uses her picture instead of the Imagine Graphics logo. Her reasoning is that she is the face behind the social media presence, and because she feels comfortable with the mix of the personal and the public in Imagine Graphics's social presence. She also feels that while people like to connect with businesses, they want to know that there is a real person behind the business, and using her face is the best way to show that. As she puts it, "Facebook is a very personal place," and businesses must make an effort to be part of that personal environment.

Another way to add a personal touch to your social network site is by showing images of the actual business and people working in it. Somer Deck (Fifth Street Public Market) says her market is more than just a collection of businesses. "It's all the faces that run it that you see here on a day-to-day basis. So that's another good opportunity to just reinforce that, to put pictures of the business owners, all these people who are here all the time."

Some businesses chose a well-known face to be the face of the business: someone who might be a local, or even national, celebrity. Brian Mason (SKP-Popcorn) uses the face of local and national celebrity and three-time contestant on the reality show *Survivor*, Rupert Boneham. Boneham is "kind of this crazy, crazy haired, tie dyed shirt wearing guy" according to Brian, and he was selected because he's from Indianapolis, where SKP is based. He has a very colorful personality, and attends a variety of promotional events for the company. Boneham's connection virtually guarantees that many people will show up at events, and so both his face and the events are promoted online.

While your business may not have access to a national celebrity, you may wish to consider asking local celebrities such as sports heroes or media personalities to be the face of your business.

Other businesses have been successful using something as simple as their pet to be the face of their business. Beth Colla and Tim Ferguson (Lake Street Creamery) filmed a series of videos in their living room that featured one of their new kittens wearing a little hat and eating a tiny ice cream cone. They posted the video on YouTube, followed by other videos of their kittens, and now the kittens Scout Junior and Speedo are the face of their business.

Encourage Interaction

A social networking site like Facebook features a "wall" where you and your customers can post content. Also, blogs have comment sections where more content can be posted. Many sites end up with numerous unrelated comments that can be interesting to read (or just spam), but indicate little interaction among people visiting the site. Without this interaction among different people, you're missing the opportunity to build a community. Communities tend to build around leaders, you and the people who are frequent visitors and participants at your site. The best leaders inspire and encourage others to be involved in the community.

In our first book, *Building Buzz to Beat the Big Boys*, we talked about social glue: something that you and your customers have in common beyond a simple interest in your business. If you sell wine and cheese, for example, your social glue might be fine dining. A bicycle store might have a social glue of fitness. If your business has a strong social glue, use it to encourage interaction at your social network site. Kelli Matthews (Café Yumm!) uses this idea in the restaurant's community-building efforts. She sees that Café Yumm!'s Facebook and Twitter sites creates what she calls "a community of interest" of people who seek healthy and delicious food, and that social media provides a place for those people to meet and engage with others like them. Given that food is such a large part of people's lives, it is natural for a restaurant to develop a community around food. It places the restaurant in the middle of someone's everyday life, and the restaurant becomes more than an occasional stop for lunch. Kelli sees customers sharing information on both Twitter and Facebook; not just information about Café Yumm! but also about recipes, healthy eating, and nutrition in general.

Similarly. Dutch Bros. Coffee's mission is to make everyone who buys coffee drinks at their outlets feel like family, and the baristas create a unique and individual customer experience. This connection comes across in their social media sites, which Adam Cuppy (Dutch Bros. Coffee) views as simply a connection to the community created by the outlets.

Sometimes the community of interest might be based around the city where your business is located. Qoola uses the city of Vancouver as their community of interest. Jesse Yu (Qoola) says that the community started with the Olympics after the event thrust the city into the international spotlight. Jesse and his team recognized some of the unique cultural aspects of the city, including its large Asian population, and made efforts to reach out and provide content to that market in their social medium. Jesse believes that their social media reflects a range of interest beyond the business, including local events, movies, and sports. As Jesse puts it, "we don't always have to talk about yogurt."

One interesting way to start conversations is to post something controversial. Utah Dave Robison (Realtor) found that people will respond more often to controversial topics than to noncontroversial ones (more on this in the next chapter). Keep in mind, though, that often people don't want to be the first person to answer a question or to comment on a controversial post. This is nothing personal against you or your content; it is merely a vagary of human nature. What you can do in this situation is, offline, ask close friends or colleagues to be the first to make a comment. Then you can respond to the comments, and visitors to your social network site will see that you indeed are there and are responding to the comments.

Another way to encourage interaction is to reward interaction, especially when you're just starting to establish your community. One of the easiest (and least expensive) ways to reward people is just to thank them (see Chapter 2 for more on thanking people). Even a quick, personal "thank you," reposted either at the social network site or in a personal email, is a type of reward. One business that does a great job of this is Sierra Trading Post. Any time a customer posts that they made a purchase, Sierra Trading Post thanks them, and then asks an additional question to keep the conversation going. For example, a customer posted she went to the store and bought back-to-school clothes and shoes for her boys, and sunglasses for herself. Sierra Trading Post thanked her, and then asked which glasses followed her home? This casual tone invites more conversations and clearly shows the personality behind the business.

When you are responding to someone, use their screen name and not their actual name so people who visit your social network site know who you are talking about. Try to keep track of some of the interests of your early visitors, and if you see they're not visiting as often, send them a message and ask them to come back, especially if there is a conversation that you think might interest them.

How will you know when people are coming together as a community? Just like in real life, people in communities seem comfortable with each other, making jokes yet being respectful of opinions. They will usually integrate screen names into their posts, meaning something in their tweet or update is meant for a particular individual. When you drop in to the community, you'll note some of the same names coming back on a regular basis. Jesse Yu (Qoola) refers to people who visit the social network site (and their stores) as VVCs: very valuable customers. These people tend to be very connected, and often online, and can be great word-of-mouth ambassadors for the store. Qoola offers another value to these VCCs: free Wi-Fi. Jesse encourages VVCs to hang out in their stores and use their Wi-Fi, without making people feel they're occupying valuable real estate. This also develops word of mouth for the store; Jesse believes that people who use their free Wi-Fi will mention that in their online conversations.

Managing Messages

Some communities start out slowly; others take off like gangbusters. Regardless, you need to make sure people know you're present and ready to communicate with them. Adam Wallace (Roger Smith Hotel) thinks that even if you have a million people reaching out to you, you should find a way to communicate back to them. That does not mean that you would communicate individually with each of them. Adam believes you should respond to everything in a way such that your community can see that the business is responsible.

As you get busy communicating, you want to be consistent in your messages. We'll talk more about this in the next chapter, but consistency is key to managing messages. One way is to create consistency in your marketing both in your social messaging and in your regular messaging. Utah Dave Robison (Realtor) uses this tactic, and he says that consistency across media allows his voice to be trusted. He says that when people on Facebook see him post on other's walls, or when people's friends post on his wall, they see it as a confirmation of a relationship. He believes people think "I have trust because my friend knows this guy. He says he's a great guy. I'm going to use him." As a result, Dave has seen an increase in leads from his Facebook page.

Having people see the valuable relationships that you have with other people is a key way to show trust. Qoola does this in a very interesting way. After doing some research on the food blogging site Urban spoon.com, Jesse Yu (Qoola) realized Vancouver had a larger number of dedicated food bloggers. According to Jesse:

> Vancouver is a foodie town. If you're into food, it's one of the best places to eat in the world. And one of the things I stated from the very beginning, as part of our strategy, was that we invited bloggers to come and listen to us one-on-one. We had blogger nights. They came in, we talked to them, we let them sample our product, and we told them, "Just write what you actually think. We're not trying to sit here and sway you in any way. You're either going to like it, or you don't." And some of them did, some of them didn't. But part of the reason I did that, was because I knew that there was just no way that, with our budget, [we could] do a traditional marketing campaign, and I'm not going to go out and spend a ton of money on fliers that are just going to be passed out, but that have a 10 cent coupon on it, for a nominal savings.

In Jesse's view, having the relationship with bloggers is a better value than a cents-off coupon. By inviting top food bloggers in Vancouver to the store, he generated positive comments from "objective" sources that built significant trust in the store.

Jillian Bisinger and Tony Zucca (Jillian Bisinger Modern Photographer) also reach out to bloggers to promote their business, particularly their business outside of their home base of Los Angeles. Jillian has reached out to people who blog about weddings in cities like Austin and New York, and has provided them with pictures from weddings that she has photographed to share on their blog. Jillian finds that this works very well since "wedding bloggers are always looking for weddings to write about." Most importantly, Jillian Bisinger Modern Photography has booked jobs from these blog posts, showing the power of word of mouth even if the blogger did not directly experience the business. How does Jillian find bloggers to contact? It is as simple as a Google search. Jillian searches using a phrase like "wedding bloggers Austin Texas," and she reaches out to the bloggers who turn up at the top of the list. These top-of-the-results-page bloggers, according to Jillian, have credibility and readership and can help her business. The record shows that she is correct.

Social media can also help build trust among infrequent customers. Erica Leaf (Imagine Graphics) had numerous customers that she didn't talk to regularly before social media came along. Having a social media presence, however, allowed her to reconnect with those infrequent customers and keeps Imagine Graphics top-of-mind with them. Having robust relationships is important to Imagine Graphics's business model because the people don't need signs and graphics frequently, and the purchase isn't an impulse buy. Having those regular conversations in social media spaces, then, allows that bond of trust to strengthen, rather than weaken, between a customer's purchases.

Managing the Community

Once your community takes off, you not only need to be part of the conversations but to also keep note of the general topics or tone of the conversations. You may need to dial some of them down, depending on what people are talking about. For some people, this means making use of the "delete" button to remove messages that are off topic or not building the brand.

This must be done judiciously, though, since you can run the risk of ruining the transparency inherent in social media by censoring comments. Deleting content signals to customers that their opinions may not matter and that the conversation itself is not authentic. Visitors have an infinite number of places that they can spend their online time, so many look for any reason to avoid adding another page or feed to their daily media diet. The Internet, by and large, is an open space, and if you're insistent on deleting everything that's not congratulatory or positive for your brand, people will migrate to somewhere else.

Building a strong community also means paying attention to what that community thinks and does. Keeping members informed about your business and getting their feedback on changes you're considering can lead to valuable insights. Think of your online community as an ever-present focus group. Work with the community so they can feel a sense of empowerment. That can be a matter of doing tasks such as suggesting user-generated content topics, like CNN's iReport Assignment Desk, which asks its users to become amateur reporters for CNN. Communities develop from the ground up, and need time to develop and flourish.

3.5 Action Idea: Survey your community every so often. Ask them to tell you what they like and don't like about the community. Invite them to email you directly or to post their comments at your social network site.

Get Others Involved

Managing the community takes time, and you need to have someone who can devote some time every day to the community. In many cases, it will be you. The community manager needs to immerse himself or herself in the community and talk to people: this is the only way relationships will develop.

Sometimes, the community manager might be someone other than you, and this is fine as long as they understand how social media works and why your business is involved in social media. He or she will be representing the business, not their own personal interests. In the next chapter, we'll talk about how to develop a message strategy that ensures that your manager is maintaining a social media identify that's positive for your brand and your online community.

That said, most of the retailers we spoke with recognize how difficult it is for a single person to be the eyes and ears for the entire business in the social media sphere. You might think about encouraging your staff to be participants in the community even if they aren't the manager. You can do this by allowing everyone access to the main accounts so that questions and concerns can be answered even if you're not available. Having a quick response is generally better than having the perfect response, and a quick response starts a dialogue that you can get involved with as soon as you can. You can also ask people to identify themselves in the screen name by their name and job title: "Wendy in Customer Service" for example, shows that Wendy is an employee of the business and also identifies where customers might be able to find her in real life.

Mark Beauchamp (Café Yumm!) found that the amount of input from people interested in his brand was more than he could practically deal with. Once his community was built, he found himself deluged with email, often containing questions about the restaurant and its products. He felt that he personally could handle communication duties for one social networking site, but he knew that in order to expand to other social media, he would need another person to deal with the additional workload. He hired a part-time social media person to do this work. This is another option that you might wish to consider as you build your social media presence. Of course, this individual must clearly understand your business mission, and you must be comfortable that he or she has an appropriate voice for your company.

Key Chapter Insights

- It will take effort and time to attract a social community, so be prepared to put make the investment.

- Interaction between visitors is critical to social media success because it creates additional content and word of mouth.

- Focus on social media sites that best fit your brand rather than trying to participate in too many approaches all at once. Determine your focus by looking at your consumers social media habits as well as your own.

- Choose one site that is your "nerve center" where you spend the majority of your effort and from which your content/approach emanates. Facebook might be your "nerve center" because of its user base, applications, and flexibility. Twitter might fill that role if you have short purchase cycles for your product/service and immediacy is critical. Your blog could be your "nerve center" if you have lots of information to share.

- Integration or cross-posting across different social platforms will help you optimize you social media audience and create more interaction.

- Use multiple avenues (friends' or neighbors' email; in-store promotion; advertising inclusion) to let people know your social site is up and running.

- Engage personally with your social audience. People want to connect with the owner/manager/leader.

- A social community succeeds because of the "social glue" that you use to keep it energized. Social glue is the common interest/end benefit that the community derives from exchange.

- Consistent messaging is critical in terms of building trust and credibility with your social community.

Getting Started

- If you are brand new to social media: Think about your own skills and interests in order to determine your nerve center. If you like to write, think about starting a blog. If you want to get an online presence up quickly, set up a Facebook page for your business. And if you think you would be most comfortable with short messages you can send out frequently, look at Twitter.

- If you are familiar with social media: Decide on your nerve center and contact the people in your current networks and ask them to follow your business site.

- If you are ready to move to the next level: Set goals regarding your community—how big do you want to get? Think about in-store promotion of your social media as well as through your other traditional media, and investigate Facebook advertising to direct people to your page.

Getting Started with Facebook

Facebook is one of the largest social networking sites on the Internet. As of April 2011, there are more than 800 million active users on Facebook, with 50 percent of active users logging on in any given day. Users spend more time on Facebook when they are online than on any other application. It is no wonder all types of businesses are joining the Facebook community.

For the local small business, the advantages of managing a Facebook profile and building a network of friends can be enormous. Facebook provides a convenient way for people to connect and share with their friends, family, and customers. You can send a friend a message, instant-message a relative, or post a link to a YouTube video to a coworker's "wall" (a kind of personal, digital bulletin board). Because friends are organized into networks and any friend in a network can see the activity of any other friend in the same network, the potential for powerful word-of-mouth marketing is tremendous. If one person posts a status (a short update of an activity) praising a new restaurant, they could influence the future dining choice of any number of their friends. This is why for a small business looking to build a strong, loyal customer base capable of generating buzz about a new deal, product, or service—all free of charge—there exists no better asset than Facebook.

A plus for small business is that most of Facebook's offerings are free of charge. Facebook does sell advertising space, and at some point, you may wish to consider purchasing ads. But to begin, setting up a page on Facebook is a great way to start using social media.

The Most Important Facebook Unit: The Friend

The largest benefit to Facebook, of course, is that it gives you access to lots of people. On Facebook, you build a "network" of "friends," and then you can have access to your friends' network.

What is a "friend" on Facebook? Friends want to be part of your personal network. When they want to affiliate with your business, they indicate they "like" your business. You can also use Facebook to search for friends. You can build a personal network of your friends, neighbors, family, and coworkers.

Most businesses have a goal to have a large number of Facebook friends indicate that they "like" your business. Large, however, is a matter of opinion: a local kitchen store might consider having 300 friends as having a large amount, while a fast-food giant might not be satisfied with 25,000 friends. You should check the number of friends that similar businesses to yours have in order to determine a good number.

A business page (known as an "Official" page on Facebook) is different from a personal page, as you will soon see, and when friends indicate they "like" your business (by clicking on the "Like" box at the top of your page), this fact gets displayed on the friend's personal page. Therefore, all the friends of those who "like" your business get exposed to your business also. It's a great way to get the word out.

Setting Goals

Before you jump on to Facebook, think about what you want to get out of Facebook. Of course, you want to have another place to connect with your customers. Here are some options of goals:

1. Increase your brand awareness: Facebook can increase overall awareness of your business by showcasing your business to potential customers. You can measure this by asking customers in your store where they heard about your business. You can also offer Facebook-only "specials" to monitor this.

2. Increase sales of a certain product or service: promoting a product on your Facebook page can lead to increased sales of a particular product or service, even if you don't offer a special deal on that item.

3. Increase visits to your other online offerings: your store webpage, blog, and/or online newsletter.

Set some short-term, mid-term and long-term goals for your Facebook page, such as:

1. In the next month, get 75 people to "like" our Facebook page.

2. In the next three months, get five new customers per month in the store because of our Facebook page.

3. In the next nine months, increase sales of a particular product featured on our Facebook page by 10 percent.

Creating a "Personal" Page

Before you set up a page for your retail business, you'll need to set up a personal page on Facebook. This is quick and easy; detailed instructions are below.

- Set up your account. Start by visiting Facebook's website: http://www .facebook.com. Enter the requested information in the signup form: your first and last names, your email address, a password that you select, your gender, and your birth date. (Facebook requires all users to provide their real date of birth to encourage authenticity and provide only age-appropriate access to content. Using privacy settings, though, you will be able to hide any information you don't want people to see.)

- Find your friends. Click the "Find Friends" button, and Facebook will search your email contacts for any potential friends. If you have 10 contacts in your Yahoo! email account, Facebook would try to match these friends to their Facebook account. That will allow you to start building your network right away.

- Complete your profile information. Your profile can include as much or as little information as you wish to share. If you enter information about your high school or company, Facebook can search for people who have also included that information in their profiles: another way to build your personal network.

- You can also search for people you know by entering their first and last names into the search toolbar at the top of the page. Facebook will list results according to how well the names match and the individual's geographic proximity to you.

- There are two ways to add someone as a friend. First, you can click on the "Add as Friend" link in the search results. Alternatively, you can visit their Facebook page and click the "Add as Friend" button on the right-hand side of their profile picture. A friend request will be sent to their inbox; both parties must agree to be friends before someone joins your personal network.

Features Overview

Each time you log on to Facebook, you'll be taken to a "Home" page where your "News Feed" will be displayed.

- The news feed displays the recent activities of your friends: it is your porthole into the lives of those in your network. You can update your own status from this page.

- Status updates are quick messages about what you are doing or other types of noteworthy information. Whether you are updating the status of your business or your personal life, you can use the "Attach" tool to attach links to other sites, photos, or video. Hint: before posting a new status, ask yourself, "Would this be something I'd want to read about someone else?"

- Next, click on the world "Profile" in the right-hand corner of the Home page, and you'll be taken to your personal profile page. While you're not required to have a personal profile page in order to acquire a business page, a personal page has several benefits. You'll be able to connect a personal face to your business, and you will be able to access your personal network to invite them to your business page.

  a. In addition to posting on the Home page, the "Wall" is where you post personal updates. Others who see your personal page can also comment on your wall. The comments/updates are made in the box that reads "What's on your mind?"

  b. The "Info" tab allows you to edit your personal information and include information about yourself that you would like others to know. You can, for example, share your favorite music, movies, and activities. Any section can be edited by clicking on the "Edit" button, a little blue pencil in the top right-hand corner of each section.

  c. The "Photos" tab allows you to upload photos. One popular Facebook activity is flipping through photos of friends. Using the Facebook uploader, you can upload an unlimited number of photos. For easy viewing, you can group photos into albums by clicking on "Create a Photo Album" in the top right-hand corner and filling in the desired fields.

Most importantly, set your privacy settings. Most people don't want their personal page visible to all 500 million Facebook users. To control access to your personal page, scroll down to the bottom of the page and click on the "Privacy" link on the bottom right-hand side. Facebook will walk you through the various privacy options you have.

Setting Up an "Official" Page for Your Business

Once you have your personal page set up, you're ready to set up a page for your business.

1. Scroll down to the bottom of your personal page and click on the link "Advertising." This will take you to the Facebook Advertising page.

2. At the very top of the page, find the green box that says "Create an Ad." Click the link underneath this that says "or manage an existing ad." This will take you to a Facebook ads overview where you will see a link to promote your Facebook page. Click on it.

3. Click on the green "Create a Page" button.

4. Fill out the requested information about your business. Click on the circle by the word "Local Business" and use the pull-down box to identify what type of business you're in. If your category isn't listed on that pull-down menu, fill in the type of business in the "Name of Other Business" Box.

5. Click on the box next to the statement "I am authorized to create this Page."

6. Enter your name in the "Electronic Signature" box.

7. Finally, click on the "Create Official Page" button.

Congratulations! You know have an Official page for your business!

When you'd like to access your new Facebook Fan page, click the "Account" tab in the upper right-hand corner, manage pages, and then the relevant page.

Now that you're at your Fan page, it's time to start sharing information and building your community. Here are four ways for you to get started.

Invite Friends to "Like" Your Page

You can easily invite friends from your personal network to "like" your Official business page.

- On the upper left-hand corner of your business page, look for the words "Suggest to Friends."

- Click on the words, and a pop-up box will be displayed listing all your friends.

- Click on the pictures of the friends you wish to invite to your Official page, and then click the "Send Invitation" button.

- An invitation will be automatically sent to your selected friends inviting them to join your fan page.

Post to Your "Wall"

Keep your fans updated with news about your store. The easy-to-use status update box is found at the top of your page. You can type directly into the box where it says, "What's on your mind?" What should be on your mind?

o   Talk about new products or service offerings.

o   Highlight the accomplishments of someone who works for you.

o   Mention sales and other promotions.

o   See Chapter 4 for other messaging ideas.

Add Photos

Adding photos of products, services, your store, and your staff can give your store a personality. Photos are also featured on your Wall when you add them.

To add photos, you'll need digital photos that you move temporarily to your computer desktop. There are a couple of different ways you can add photos. One way is via your "Wall":

•   Click the "Wall" tab.

•   Enter something about the photo in your update box: "Here's some new merchandise that just arrived today."

•   Click on the photo icon.

•   Click on the words "Upload a Photo."

•   Click on the "Browse" button to get a list of photos on your desktop

•   Click on the photo you want to upload.

•   Click on the "Share" button, and you're done.

Add Links

You can easily add links to other web pages that might be of interest to your customers. For example, you can link to an outside review of a product that you sell from a site like CNET (which rates electronics products). Here is how:

•   Click the "Wall" tab.

•   Enter something about the link in the status update box: "Here's a review of a product that you might be interested in."

- Look for the word "attach" immediately under the status update box.
- Click on the "Link" icon, which looks like a piece of paper with a thumbtack in it.
- Type in the URL of the site you wish to share. You can also cut and paste the URL; just be sure that you don't repeat "http" twice.
- Click the blue "Share" box.

Add Events

You can quickly add notifications about events that you will hold in your store. You can also add events that you support that might be outside of your store, such as a community bake sale or theater production. Here's how:

- Click the "Wall" tab.
- Enter a brief description of the event in the status update box: "We're having an in -store demonstration of a new product!"
- Look for the word "Attach" immediately under the status update box.
- Click on the "Calendar" icon, which looks like a page from a calendar.
- Enter information about the event in the pop-up box: the name of the event and the date.
- Click the blue "Share" box.
- The event will also appear on the left-hand column: scroll down to see a list of all the events you enter.

Tips for Successful Facebooking

- Spend a little time on Facebook and see what types of messages your friends like and respond to. Don't fill your Wall with self-promotional posts; work to engage customers in the space.
- Visit the Official pages of your neighboring businesses and your competitors to see what types of information they provide and what type of response they are getting.
- Review the messaging suggestions in Chapter 4.
- Be visible: post something on your wall at least once a day.

4

Social Messaging: Best Practices for Social Communication

> It's literally like stepping into a room with all these people talking, and you're going from conversation to conversation. How do you know what these people are doing next week? You don't, and in order to remain relevant you have to always be aware of what's going on at that moment. Then, how do you leverage your business within that conversation? You just don't barge into someone else's conversation with someone, and say, "Hey, by the way, I have a yogurt shop."
>
> —Jesse Yu (Qoola)

You've thought about your objectives, you've decided where you want to have a presence, and you've established your social media accounts. Now what? Like any new relationship, the first few days, or weeks, of using social media are great—you have all kinds of things to talk about, and you're intrigued by the newness of it all. But after the novelty wears off, many small business owners flounder with wondering what to say, how often to post content, and in general, how to handle the social media communication.

In this chapter, we'll describe the best practices for communicating in the social media space, including generating ideas for messages, planning a campaign, matching message to medium, and mixing up the voices.

Use Your Business Mission and Vision to Tell Good Stories

One thing that many businesses forget about social media is that it is social. One recent study of online users of social networks (Gangharbatla and Sheehan 2010) showed that the primary reason people use social media is to connect and interact with friends and family. Far down the list, people told us they used social media to get information. So in order to be successful in the social media world, you have to participate in some of the basic ways that people make connections with one another: by telling good stories. These stories should be based on what is centrally important to your business.

Stories and Social Glue

This is likely to be related to your social glue: the one thing you, your business, and your customers have in common. Social glue should be a bigger, broader topic than just your business (see our book *Building Buzz to Beat the Big Boys* for lots more about social glue). The Roger Smith Hotel in New York, for example, is run by James Knowles, who transformed a hotel from a generic, nondescript spot into an art hotel. The hotel integrates artwork throughout the building. The walls of the main restaurant display several murals, and handcrafted sculptures are featured in the hallway and lobby. Events hosted at the hotel have art themes. By extension, the art becomes a centerpiece of some of the marketing messages, and it also provides an atmosphere that is welcoming and recognizable to guests. Hence, art is the Roger Smith Hotel's social glue. Focusing their stories on art provides an easy way to create interesting and engaging content online. Adam Wallace at the Roger Smith Hotel describes it this way:

> It's crucial to have a story to tell. I think a lot of hotels and small businesses in general that are used to just promoting their business in a very traditional way only talk about their product. Talking about your product is only interesting for so long, and it's not very shareable. So if we can have a bigger story happening at the hotel with the art, and the community, and the events, we've created a whole huge story that is changing every day, I think a lot of businesses struggle; they don't really know what they're going to talk about, so then they just talk

about their rates, or they just talk about their features and benefits of their product and that's fine, for a little bit, but there's definitely a bigger story that is important to engage with.

In order to develop your social glue and to engage customers with stories, it is important to go back to your business mission and vision. Think of that business mission and vision as a base from which to build all your other messages. Café Yumm!'s mission, for example, focuses on making food that is delicious, nourishing, and beautiful. They use that information to determine their posting topics. This philosophy allows them to have a degree of flexibility in the actual topics that they talk about, but at the same time, it gives them the ability to always tie the messages back to the food that they offer. Dutch Bros. Coffee has a mission statement composed of three core values: quality, speed, and service. Their messages all focus on one of these three areas, and speak from the perspective of the individual customer experience.

4.1. Action Idea: Determine your social glue. Think broadly about your business mission, vision, and offerings. You don't sell pet food; you share nutrition information for people's beloved pets. You don't sell spaghetti and rigatoni; you host an evening of Italian culture. You don't sell coffee; you are a familiar face during a hectic day.

Try to talk about your social glue in a way that differs from other businesses. For example, many companies focus on their environmentally friendly business practices as part of their social glue. At Café Yumm! for example, the restaurants use green materials in fabricating counters and tables. However, they rarely focus their messages around this, as they feel their audience is smart enough to be able to find information about green materials on their own. Instead, Café Yumm! focuses specifically on why they believe these practices tie into their core values of beautiful, delicious, and nourishing food. In that way, they build the community still using their core message as a base. It makes the café's choices more personal to its customers.

What can you build your stories around? Look at what makes your business unique and interesting to other people. The Vancouver yogurt store Qoola looks at their unique point of difference relative to the competition. Jesse Yu (Qoola) uses fresh yogurt rather than powdered, which most of his competitors use. Because of this, Jesse uses their social media presence to educate the public about the taste and nutritional differences between fresh and powdered yogurt. According to Jesse, the business makes a habit of anytime they have superlatives to talk about their product, they use the word fresh. This consistency will help connect the Qoola brand with this key benefit of freshness, and gives people information to share when they are talking about Qoola with others. Jilian Bisinger and Tony Zucca (Jillian Bisinger Modern Photography) use their outgoing personalities and their unique vision in terms of photography to tell stories that engage potential customers. Daniel Pollard (Pelican Brew Pub and Restaurant) uses their unique location right on the Pacific Ocean to share customer stories and talk about fun events.

Stories with Passion

Justin Stobb (All Wheel Drive Auto) believes that whatever their social glue, businesses must show their passion for the topic. He believes people want to come back to his social network sites for new information because they know he's excited to share the information with them. Justin and his staff truly love fixing cars and they love Subarus, and sharing information and their passion makes customers see them as the experts in this area. Similarly, Adam Cuppy (Dutch Bros. Coffee) sees that the social glue for the coffee shack business is a unique and individual customer experience. Social media, then, becomes the way to continue the connection between the customer and the barista, who is familiar with his or her "regulars" and the beverages they regularly order.

Many businesses get passionate about an event that is happening, and increase their posting frequency around that event. For example, we noticed increases in posts by bicycle stores during the Tour de France, and increases in posts by sports bars during all-star games and during football season. Posting during these events is a great way for businesses to show their passion and to energize their social media presence. The risk is that after the event, the business's posts will fall off. It is important to remember to keep the excitement and passion going even when a big event is not happening.

Simple, Specific Stories

Having a focused message that runs exclusively is a key way to make sure the story gets told, and that you see the results you wish to see. Many new users of social media for marketing purposes get overwhelmed with telling all their stories in all types of social media. It will work better if you focus one story in one medium. Paco Miller (Tia Juana's) was successful with this tactic when he introduced "Taco Tuesday" at his restaurants. When he started Taco Tuesday, he sent one tweet per week for several months focusing on the event, with no other messages on Twitter. The restaurant has experienced exponential growth that night.

Stories That Build Community

We talked about leveraging the local aspects of the business in the previous chapter on building community, but that can be the centerpiece of your messages as well. Like many small businesses, the record store CD World uses its position as a local, non-franchised business to tell stories. The store can quickly embrace new artists, and sell not only music, but T-shirts and posters. Hosting in-store events when bands come to town has turned into a boon, as they are the last record shop to offer a venue for bands, unlike the CD section at Target. The Tattered Cover bookstore also uses their independent status as a positioning strategy. They're the largest independent store in the central United States, making them a destination for famous authors from around the world. They do their best to maintain a healthy balance between promoting the book signings of famous authors and those of local authors to ensure they're reaching as many people in the area as possible.

The other value of building stories around your vision and mission is that the story, and hence your brand message, is consistent, and your identity will be clear. You avoid the pitfall of publishing a variety of different and inconsistent tweets or statuses that can confuse customers. Some retailers use the idea of a media calendar: a tool that allows them to plan out events and subsequent messages over the course of several weeks. The calendar allows retailers to have a "big picture" view and to connect the messages of inshore events to the larger mission statement.

4.2 Action Idea: Think of different types of stories you could tell and integrate them into your editorial calendar. One week, talk about special events (perhaps recap an event). During the next week, talk about something related to your social glue. The next week, perhaps an employee has a story to relate.

This type of editorial calendar should not be adhered to so strictly that other types of messages are excluded. One of the advantages of social media is its immediacy, which means that it is important to connect messages not only to the vision, but to what is happening right now.

Create Promotions That Are Timely, Relevant, and Immediate

For many people, the key benefit of social media is letting friends and family know, at this very moment, what they are doing. This immediacy presents a challenge to small business owners, who find that they must balance this need for immediacy with the needs of running their own businesses on a day-to-day basis. How do small businesses manage to create timely messages regularly?

The simplest way to do this is to use social media to talk about what is happening at your business today, tomorrow, and in the weeks to come. Lisa Hartwick (Hartwick's Kitchen Store) plans a lot of in-store events and uses social media to both promote the events and do a "recap" of the events after they happen. One recurring event is a monthly baking contest in which customers bring in a specific baked good that they've created. At the start of the month, Lisa announces the baking category (one month the contest involves brownies, the next month croissants) on both Twitter and Facebook, and then follows up by reminding customers via Twitter up until the contest deadline. Then she uses Facebook and Twitter to announce the winners.

Patty Miller (The Tattered Cover bookstore) and William Kennedy (CD World) also use social media to announce events. These stores regularly host visits from authors and artists from around the country, so these visits are special opportunities for customers to interact with their favorite artists and, by extension, the business. Customers are encouraged to "live tweet," meaning they send updates from their laptop or mobile phone as the event is happening, which fuels word of mouth and can draw big crowds almost instantly. Both stores use social media to announce new releases; CD World also announced other types of entertainment choices, such as new movies opening in the area. The stores also announce re-releases, some of which can be exclusive, as when Iggy Pop released a record on purple vinyl, which was available only at a select few record stores. In this way, these stores have turned into an information hub about the entertainment venues in the market where they operate.

Jesse Yu (Qoola) has a different take on immediacy. Qoola uses Vancouver's notoriously bad weather in the winter as a promotional tool. When it is raining outside and business is slow, Qoola uses Twitter to invite customers to come in and tell them that "rain sucks" in return for a free topping on their yogurt. This sense of immediacy, of being in the know, helps customers feel like they are part of your business, which encourages them to share information about your business with others, thus starting and maintaining the word-of-mouth process.

Pelican Brew Pub, located on the beach in Pacific City, Oregon, created a T-shirt commemorating an annual surfboard event. They promote the T-shirt (and a special beer brewed specifically for the event) on their Facebook page, including an email address for placing orders (they could have just as easily placed a website link). Since the pub is located in a vacation community, it is likely that some people who have recently visited the pub and could not travel to the event will purchase the T-shirt to keep their connection to the pub and to the vacation experience.

Understanding customer segments can be very helpful in creating timely messages. Paco Miller (Tia Juana's) has several distinct customer segments: lunch diners, happy-hour patrons, dinner customers, and nightclubbers. He has found that each group welcomes messages directed to their interests, but dislikes messages directed to the other segments. He also found that nightclubbers attending "hip-hop night" disliked receiving messages about salsa dancing night. To address this, he set up unique Facebook pages for these different experiences, and also makes sure that text messages and tweets are directed to the specific subsegment that will most interest them.

The possibilities are endless. Burke's Bar, in Yonkers, New York, tweeted a special offer of $1 draft beers on the night LeBron James announced what NBA team he would join. This connects to sports-oriented social glue. Blue Moon Burgers in Seattle and Marche Restaurant in Eugene, Oregon, tweet about shakes, ice tea, and sodas during heat waves. In that same vein, the Hotel Lucia in Portland, Oregon, offers a $99 room rate via Twitter when the temperature reaches 99 degrees. The restaurant Naples Tomato in Florida is located near a nature preserve, and it connects special offers to the special events at the preserve (one tweet announced that a special orchid, the Ghost Orchid, was in bloom and offered a special in connection with that).

The Social Media Cocktail Party

Conversations come from being both timely and topical. Good social media cocktail party conversations are fresh and connected with what other people are talking about that moment. Like at any cocktail party, you don't want to be seen as the arrogant bore who only knows how to talk about yourself. Your goal is fit your business into the conversations that are currently happening.

It all starts with the tone. An informal, conversational voice will ensure that your audience knows there's a real, thoughtful person behind the computer at your business. The overall feeling needs to be spontaneous, even if you've spent a long time thinking about what you're going to say. Adam Cuppy (Dutch Bros. Coffee) thinks of his company as another friend in his list of friends on Facebook. He talks as a friend to another friend, not as a company to a customer.

> **4.3 Action Idea:** Read your posts out loud before you post them. Does what you just read sound like something you would say in person to a friend or a customer? If yes, go ahead and post it! If not, try again until your post sounds like you are having a natural conversation.

Establishing this type of consistent tone is important. The ultimate goal is to have something that is going to be interesting for other people to hear, and ultimately worth sharing in the eyes of your audience. This is how word of mouth starts.

Successful retailers agree that not anything that seems overly managed and processed will work in the social network sphere. The "overly managed" category of messages includes using any type of automated message, or messages—like promotions—that are repeated over and over again without any regard for people who might be paying attention (they probably won't be). Social networking sites like Twitter will allow you to create an automated response that is delivered to people who chose to follow you. While it is great to recognize new followers, these automated messages are missing the personal touch and can be annoying. Rich and Kim Gans (Sweet Flour Bakery) adamantly refuse to use any type of automated messages, and like many other business owners, they make a point of personally responding to people so their own personalities shine through. Their messages are consistently lighthearted and upbeat, which matches the tone they wish to see in their business.

How can you be a good partygoer at the social media cocktail party? Jesse Yu (Qoola) encourages businesses to provide some kind of benefit or insight that people find beneficial in their lives. Trey Pitsenger (Golden Gecko Garden Center) focuses on whatever is on the mind of the garden center industry. His messages react often to what is happening in the industry and how it might affect him, his customers, and other small business owners. So when wholesalers close, or large competitors change their practices, Trey gives his perspective. He finds that talking about what is on his mind, from an informed, professional perspective, resonates with his audience.

What both these businesses have in common is that the people involved with social media listen to the conversations happening around them. This is another great characteristic of someone who is successful at the social media cocktail party; someone who takes the time to tap into the existing conversations and add to them. They are also passionate about what they believe in, and this passion encourages others to express their passion as well.

Think Visually

Many discussions of social media messaging start and end with text. The written word is great, but images, photographs, drawings, and perhaps even a video are ultimately much more engaging. All these visual elements are a great way to quickly connect an emotion to the other information you're providing.

It is odd to imagine that it used to take a high level of technical expertise to add images to a web page. Today, most social media, including Facebook and Twitter, allow users to quickly and easily upload pictures, videos, and other types of content other than simple text. This will enrich your "feed" and give your customers even more to talk about.

In the most general terms, your images will be of people, places, and things. All three categories can have a place in your social media usage.

The "people" category is a rich category, as you can consider posting pictures of yourself, your staff, and your customers. Rich and Kim Gans (Sweet Flour Bakery) take a photograph of the "Customer of the Day" that they feature on their website and in their social media. Recently, the customers included a two-year-old boy named Lucas enjoying a cookie filled with candy. It's very likely, then, that Lucas's family will email that link out to their friends and family.[1] Another blog post featured a customer named Nick, who was referred to as one of the bakery's "top Twitter fans." This alerts customers that Sweet Flour has a Twitter presence, but does so in a somewhat unobtrusive way. Both of these blog posts direct potential customers to the business's website and, eventually, to the bricks-and-mortar business itself. Jillian Bisinger and Tony Zucca (Jillian Bisinger Modern Photography) post selected images from weddings and family portrait shoots using all their social media, and direct people to their blog and website for more information. Adam Cuppy (Dutch Bros. Coffee) encourages baristas and managers to post "shout outs" to their regular customers on their Facebook wall, including pictures of the customers in their cars as they wait for their coffee. Brad Niva (Rogue Wilderness Adventures) hired a professional photographer to take pictures of the beautiful Rogue River Valley, where his business is located. He shares these photos, which includes customers having fun using equipment with the company's logo, with magazines and hotels and other vacation-oriented people. The value is clear: his logo is subtle, yet always seen in these photographs.

> **4.4 Action Idea:** What is something fun that happens at your business? Does it tell customers something about your business? Then think about making a video of that!

In addition to images of people, think about including images of places: your business, the environment around your business, and even the city where your business is. Images

---

[1] It is important that you have your customers' permission to use their pictures, and it never hurts to get them to sign a simple photograph release: a single piece of paper that says "I give permission to [store name] to use my image in their online communications. I also allow them to use images of the minors listed below." Then have a space for them to sign and to list the names of any children under the age of 18.

of place can be very evocative. Somer Deck (Fifth Street Public Market) identified key benefits of using images in her social media messages:

> Any time I try and do any sort of campaign, it's always more important for me to implement pictures than it is necessarily text, because customers identify with that. They identify with our logo, with the fountain (that is at the center of the market). That's just such an important part of who we are, is showing that it is a lifestyle; it's not just a place where you come and buy jeans or kitchenware. You can do all of those things, for sure, but you can also bring your kids down here and play with the ducks in the fountain.

The Fifth Street Public Market also does a great job of taking pictures of the changing seasons, which serves to remind customers that as the seasons change, they need new merchandise for the new season that is, of course, available at the Market. The Sierra Trading Post sells equipment for camping and other outdoor activities. They actively solicit Facebook fans to post pictures of their outdoor travels to the Sierra Trading Post Facebook page. In addition, they actively comment on the photographs and occasionally offer a contest awarding a $50 gift certificate for the best posted picture.

The final category of photographs is the category of "things," which can encompass the items that your business sells. "Things" can be a little tricky, particularly in the food area. While many restaurants may be eager to photograph entrees, food is notoriously difficult to photograph, and it is possible that the food will end up looking inedible or unappetizing. That's not the image you want for your business! For food establishments, consider hiring a professional photographer, or consider using photos of either drinks or desserts, both of which tend to be more appealing in a photograph.

Video is also becoming an option for many businesses, especially given the ease of using technology like Flip Cams and other small, point-and-shoot cameras. Some firms take this a step beyond amateur video by collaborating with production companies. One example is the Roger Smith Hotel in New York City, who works with the Sandman Productions team to create videos for the hotel's blog, Roger Smith Life. Adam Wallace (Roger Smith Hotel) described one of the videos this way:

We did a video of Henry, our dog, at the hotel, him making his bed, and we got a huge amount of hits on You Tube, and it went sort of viral, and it was just sort of an iPhone shot video. Also a lot of the videos that other people have done here got a lot of buzz. Video gets a huge amount of attention.

Videos also feature footage of different events at the hotel. They've created so many videos that they developed a Roger Smith Hotel YouTube channel, further extending their reach into the social media world.

Della Mendenhall (Gillespie Florist) thinks videos are great for showing her ever-changing and beautiful stock. She often takes a video camera into the flower cooler to show what flowers are available that day, and posts the video on her Facebook page and at her Google Local site. Brad Niva (Rogue Wilderness Adventures) puts up videos of some of his special trips, such as trips where dogs are welcome on the rafts. He finds that videos encourage people to stay on the site longer. He actually tested the value of a 30-second video compared to a four-minute video, and found the 30-second video was watched much more frequently than the longer video.

Beth Colla and Tim Ferguson's (Lake Street Creamery) YouTube videos of their kittens were used to generate excitement about their new business and generated a huge response on YouTube. In fact, their videos "went viral": that is, they spread around the Internet by being reposted at blogs and websites and, in a huge viral coupe, at the popular website the Huntington Post. Now, customers expect Beth and Tim to bring the kittens in the truck, and are often disappointed when they find that the kittens stayed home.

Like our other business owners, Beth and Tim have no idea why their videos become so popular but think it might have been due to a few things: the videos are fairly short (about a minute or so long), they are humorous (kittens wearing hats and eating ice cream), the kittens are beautiful, and the videos make people laugh.

There are a few cautionary tales about using video. Even if you don't use an expensive production company, videos still require more work that people often realize. To do well, they need to be properly edited. While editing is relatively easy if you have a basic knowledge of your computer's software, it can also take time away from other activities. Adam Cuppy

(Dutch Bros. Coffee) warns about the "American Idol" mentality of videos: businesses can spend so much time trying to create the one video that will explode onto the Internet, and yet that energy might be better spent on other communications. Finally, it is very difficult to get a video removed from YouTube, so while you'll have control over video on your social media site, you have little control over what is on YouTube.

Be Controversial

We previously mentioned how Trey Pitsenger (Golden Gecko Garden Center) talks about his own personal perspective about the nursery industry in his posts. Occasionally, someone will disagree with his opinion, creating controversy. Many small businesses may shy away from being opinionated for fear that it will alienate customers who don't share the same opinion. However, most small businesses find that a little bit of controversy can be helpful in energizing their readers. Pitsenger, for example, finds that "posts that are controversial always get a bigger reaction. The industry needs to shine a light on issues that have been hiding in the wings."

Utah Dave Robison (Realtor) used to focus only on posting noncontroversial information, and found that while occasionally he'd get some positive comments, on the whole, there wasn't much interaction taking place between his audience. He does like to keep his messages positive, because it suits his personality better and his posts come off as enthusiastic and fun-loving, just like he is in real life. However, he has found that the controversial posts generate significantly more reader comments and interactions. He says that "anything that stirs up controversy is really interesting. Anything that someone has an opinion on that they can be passionate about will get the most responses."

One of Della Mendenhall's (Gillespie Florist) most visited posts involved her opinions on a practice called drop shipping, which is very controversial in the florist industry (it involves having florists order flowers from a central location for delivery, with the florist never seeing the flowers before they were delivered to the customer). Della's florist does not use drop shipping, and has heard many stories from customers about bad experiences from the practice. Her post on the practice generated a lot of comments from both industry professionals and customers, and often shows up on Google searches for drop-shipped flowers (see Chapter 5 for more on search).

Celebrate Customer Involvement

Being controversial is one way to encourage customer involvement. Getting customers to participate adds to the content on your social media site, and in general, the more content on a site, the more people will come back to visit the site and think about becoming engaged on your site as well. There are many ways to encourage this involvement. Adam Cuppy (Dutch Bros. Coffee) encourages baristas to connect with customers on social media; using simple messages like "I hope Susie at the DMV had a great day" will often generate a return comment (and future visits to the site) from Susie. Asking questions also generates responses: asking about a favorite beverage on a hot or cold day, a favorite business experience, a great travel trip, or anything related to your social glue and what your business sells, will often get some great conversations going. Similarly, ask people what they want your business to carry: in this way, your social network site becomes a virtual focus group to learn how to improve your business.

> 4.5 Action Idea: Sometimes customer's conversations go a bit off topic. What should you do? Go back to the "cocktail party" analogy: good conversations often bounce from topic to topic. Let it go for a while, but then post a question or comment about your business to get people back on track.

Think about encouraging customers to also post pictures and videos that they have taken. Adam Cuppy's (Dutch Bros. Coffee) experience is that people like to make videos about brands they love: he has seen YouTube videos of customer-created commercials as well as video captures of customers' interactions at the drive-through windows at Dutch Bros. This is a way to engage the type of online users that Forrester media refers to as "creators," people who like to express themselves and their creativity online. Of course, there's a risk that the quality won't be as good as you wish, but always remember that you have the ultimate veto power over what gets posted to your own site.

JP Poloway (Mountain Trek) gets involvement the "low tech" way: Mountain Trek provides guests with a comment sheet at the end of their stay where guests are invited to write a testimonial for the company. She then uses these testimonials on both their website and their Facebook site.

Dealing with Special Offers

Some retailers offer "Facebook-only" or "Twitter-only" specials on those media. The value of this strategy is that you can quickly measure the reaction to the message in terms of consumer interest and sales. This is especially helpful if you're using more than one type of social network and want to get a quick idea of the involvement and engagement in each medium.

4.6 Action Idea: Make special offers that you promote on social media good for a very limited time: for the day only, or for the next 24 hours. That way you can track the results and be able to focus on different products or services regularly.

Robbie Vitrano (Naked Pizza) uses a special offer code that's available only through Twitter. That way, he can easily tell how the people buying pizza found them. Other restaurants do this in a more casual way—they post a tweet that says "mention you follow us on Twitter and get a free appetizer" or "ask for our Twitter special and get two drinks for the price of one." Many restaurants especially use this tactic on slower days to see if quick tweets stimulate a response.

Roger Smith Hotel in New York City has another example for slow times. In one slow period, they did a promotion called Roger Rooms, only on Twitter. Adam Wallace describes the promotion this way:

> We basically gave away a room a night, for the month of January, and we didn't set a strict plan or the entire month, saying this is what we're going to do, and this is how it's going to work, and this is how it's going to be successful, because we didn't know what's going to be successful. We're doing giveaways via Twitter ... one of the room giveaways was, pick a number between 1 and 1,000; whoever gets closest wins a free room. And then we did a video the next day where we picked a card out of a deck, and [asked people to] guess what card it was. And whoever got closest won.

Both of those promotions were very successful. One of them generated 453 additional tweets, creating a strong amount of buzz. An important aspect of that type of promotion was that it was very simple for people to participate in, and this lack of complexity encourages all types of people to get involved with the brand.

Retail stores can use these techniques as well. Lisa Hartwick uses Twitter to promote an item of the week—a special price on one item that is advertised only on Twitter. When people come in to ask for it, she can quickly measure the response from the tweet. Hartwick's also uses Craigs-List, which gets little attention in discussion of social media but is a great resource. CraigsList is an online network of communities that are loosely structured around cities and states. The centerpiece of these communities is free online classified advertisements, with sections devoted to jobs, housing, personals, for sale, services, community, gigs, resumes, and discussion forums. Lisa told us about how she strategically uses CraigsList:

> I just knew that I had some discounted blow-out items I had customers right away off of CraigsList within that first week . . . that specifically came into look at that product. So it was very effective for us. My deals weren't outrageous deals but it was like 30 percent off, 40 percent off. I did a couple of espresso machines. And then I did some very nice German cookware. And so my stuff probably on CraigsList seemed expensive, but for the quality and the deal that was being offered it was a very good deal. But it wasn't 50, 75 percent off stuff. . . . I absolutely know that the people that were looking at the cookware had never been in. And there's probably five people that hadn't been in that came in to look at that. I thought that was a very good number for a quick little posting.

Utah Dave Robison finds that other businesses are eager to provide him with prizes to give away, and he matches the item to the appropriate social network. On his Facebook page, he has given away concert tickets, Chick-fil-A coupons, and passes to the local Parade of Homes show. He encourages interaction in order for people to win the tickets. Sometimes this works, but sometimes it doesn't. In one promotion, he asked people to call his office and sing in order to get the freebies. After a poor response, he decided to instead stick to interaction at the social network site.

Not all retailers agree with "Twitter-only" or "Facebook-only" promotions. Adam Cuppy (Dutch Bros. Coffee) encourages customers to follow Dutch Bros. using social media and also wants customers to sign up for email newsletters and text messages from the company. In return, he promises that customers will get coupons and discounts that they can use and share with friends and family. Adam sees a value in promoting them all as one unit, so that the same messages are seen in all their promotional media. He wants customers to feel valued regardless of the types of messages they chose to receive, and this consistent promotional strategy is a great way to do that.

The Value of Employee Participation

One of the biggest challenges for all small businesses is finding the time to nurture your online community. We discussed this a bit at the end of Chapter 3, and we're revisiting it here because including your employees in your tweeting can be valuable and important.

At Qoola, the business is considering having all employees tweet for a very strategic reason: employees are on the front line of noticing how much inventory is likely to go to waste if it doesn't get sold. At a food company like Qoola, having fresh ingredients is paramount. If there is an abundance of mango in one store, for example, the manager could send a tweet that says "Free mango toppings for anyone coming in between now and closing today." Jesse Yu (Qoola) believes this is a way to both manage inventory and make the business "real-time."

Good social marketers recognize is that it may be difficult to just turn employees loose to represent your company in the social media sphere without a clear understanding of the role of social media in the company. Additionally, your staff needs to understand how their social media work fits in with the other work that they're expected to do. Finally, the staff should realize the difference between information that is interesting to them and information that is interesting to your followers. Erica Leaf's (Imagine Graphics) ideal situation is that many employees would be tweeting from their business. To do this, she would have individuals set up business accounts and use the Imagine Graphics logo as part of the avatar.

Brad Niva (Rogue Wilderness Adventures) had one employee volunteer to take over the Facebook site. Brad readily agreed, and now that one employee (who also leads rafting and hiking trips) updates the Facebook site with photos and videos of the company. Brad has complete trust in this employee and his decisions, and believes that this may attract younger people to the business.

William Kennedy (CD World) is sometimes surprised that his employees—young, tech-savvy people—rarely think about using social media to send out messages on behalf of the store. He encourages his employees, when they're visiting message boards for the bands they are interested in, to refer to CD World and their social media presence. He often finds, though, that his employees don't see the connection between their hobby and their job. He is constantly reminding them to mention CD World in their Internet travels, and encourages employees to post on the store's Facebook page.

One company at which participating in social media is an important aspect of people's jobs is the Roger Smith Hotel, where the CEO wants the entire staff to have a voice online. According to Adam Wallace:

> People are really interested in the people behind the business, and the personality behind the business. And you know, (the hotel) hires good people, and encourages them to have a voice online, and I think that really creates a personality to the business that a lot of other businesses try and hide.

Adam believes that great messages can come from the "front-line" employees who are taking advantage of being able to share what is happening right now at the hotel. With so many people using social media for the Roger Smith Hotel, a big part of Adam's job is to monitor the channels and track the involvement. Certain employees are centers of interactions, particularly the restaurant manager Emile, as Adam notes:

> Emile talks to a lot of our regulars that come into the restaurant, and into the bar, and lets them know that he's on Twitter, and they—you know, they communicate to him that way, and there's a bartender who's on Twitter now, our general manager, our owner, our assistant general manager, our chef, so it's—you know, there's a bigger culture that we've cultivated within the hotel.

This makes perfect sense for a business that lives and dies by its service, but it may not be for everyone. Some owners may be hesitant to have the entire staff sharing thoughts and ideas, and some employees may spend more time with social media than they do with customer service. Regardless, it is important that you help people understand what is appropriate and what is not. Adam Wallace puts it this way:

> We just teach people, if you're going to use these channels, don't say anything that you wouldn't say to the owner or to a guest in the lobby, or to a reporter. If employees are going to talk badly about where they work, or say things that might not be compliant with the company, it's better to have it at least channeled and monitored from that standpoint. So if you say anything sort of out of line, we'll know it, maybe faster than the public can even know it, so we can respond, if they went that route. But I think, more importantly is letting these people go, and letting them say what's on their mind, and spread the word.

Adam Cuppy (Dutch Bros. Coffee) agrees with the idea of helping baristas and managers understand the voice of the company, and so provides sample scripts and conversation starters to their baristas, along with ideas about how to encourage interaction online.

Key Chapter Insights

- Social media is about being social. Focus on telling stories, not just posting information. The stories should relate your community's "social glue" the common interest/mission that your community shares.
- Some stories can be about your people or about changes in your business. People like to be connected to the people they see and they place they visit. Include visuals whenever possible.
- Use an editorial calendar to develop a consistent messaging effort. List the types or categories of information or posting you want to provide, and then determine items for each week or month in advance.
- Talk to your community not as the business owner, but as a new friend they have just met at a cocktail party.

- Videos should be fun and entertaining, not just informational. Wear your consumer hat; you want to be entertained while learning.
- Make incentives in your social community unique from other "hard-copy" offers, either in terms of duration or focus in a particular area related to a discussion or information being provided.
- Your staff can be a community-building asset if they clearly understand their role and your expectations of them.

Getting Started

- If you're brand new to social media: Think about your specific social glue and what types of messages you should be sending out through your social media.
- If you're familiar with social media: Regularly ask questions on your social media site, and start to notice what types of questions generate the most response.
- If you're ready to move to the next level: Experiment with photographs and videos to add an extra bit of excitement to your site.

Getting Started with Twitter

Twitter is an example of a microblogging application that is simple to use, easy to navigate, and a great place to start for those interested in using social media. Microblogging differs from traditional blogging in that the content of the posted message is typically much smaller in size. Twitter is the leading microblogging service, with about 75 million users worldwide as of March 2011.

How Twitter Works

When you register for a free account with Twitter (http://www.twitter.com), you get a personal home page where you can post an unlimited number of "tweets," the Twitter term for status updates. However, what you type won't matter unless someone is listening. That's where followers come in. People can "follow" you, meaning they opt in to see your tweets displayed on their personal home page. Likewise, you may follow other people, and by doing so, you will see all of their tweets on your personal home page. For example, movie star Ashton Kutcher follows 218 people on Twitter, but is followed by well over three million. While it is unlikely you'll achieve such results (we can't all be celebrities), there are a number of ways to attract more followers, which we will discuss later in this chapter.

Twitter also offers several ways to communicate with others on Twitter beyond simple tweets. The most popular, the re-tweet (RT for short), allows one user to forward the tweet of another user to their own network of followers. The RT is a powerful tool for word-of-mouth marketing that we will discuss later.

Lastly, you do not have to be at a computer to use Twitter. The service is available on cell phones (you can text tweets), and for some smartphones, the iPhone and Palm Pre in particular, you can download specialized Twitter applications to make it possible to tweet wherever you go. Two of the more popular third-party applications are HootSuite (http://www .hootsuite.com) and TweetDeck (http://www.tweetdeck.com). These third-party applications offer different ways to organize and track activities while using Twitter.

Creating a Twitter Account

1. Visit http://www.twitter.com/ and click the link "Sign Up Now."

2.   Enter the required information. Remember, your username will be how fellow tweeters recognize you. We suggest using your business name if it is available; you may have to shorten it a bit to meet the Twitter requirements.

3.   After you click Submit, you will be asked if you'd like to import your contacts from your email account. If you have contacts that you would like Twitter to locate for you automatically, use this tool. Otherwise, click "Skip this step."

4.   If you would like to follow some of Twitter's favorite people, select or deselect from the list and click "OK" on the next screen. If not, click "Skip this step."

5.   Congratulations! You now have your own account.

Your Twitter Home Page

Your personal home page will be your primary interface when you use the Twitter web page. From here you can post new tweets, read the tweets of those you follow, and discover the hottest topics on Twitter at any moment. Here are the highlights:

- *The status box*: Here you can enter your tweet. Because they must be short (140 characters or less), focus on creating interesting, succinct messages for your audience. Anything over the character limit will be cut off.

- *The feed*: The feed is the area where you can see the tweets of all of your followers, as well as your own. You can filter this feed to only see @replys, DMs, or tweets that mention a certain keyword.

- *The tweetometer*: Here you can track how many people you follow, how many are following you, and how many tweets you've posted. Don't obsess too much over the second column; the quality of your followers (whether they are potential customers or just random) is far more important than a high number.

- *The interface*: Keep track of how many people have mentioned you in one of their tweets with an @reply (more information on this follows later in this chapter). Also, you can view an inbox of your direct messages, sent and received. Like the name implies, direct messages are private tweets to a single user.

- *The trend list*: This list will give you a snapshot of the hottest topics on Twitter, measured by the amount that a keyword or string of words, like "windows 7," are mentioned in people's tweets. You can also search for a specific term using the search tool. For example, if you wanted to connect with alpaca farmers, you could find all the tweets containing that term.

Customizing Your Account

Twitter gives you a few tools to add a personal touch to your page. Take this as an opportunity to have some fun creating a warm, welcoming digital environment.

1. *Change your account photo*: The default account photo is a little bird. Here's how to change it.

    a. At the top right corner of the page, click "Settings."
    b. Click the tab that says "Picture."
    c. Upload your image from your desktop, and you are done!

2. *Change the background of your page*: If you do not like the default Twitter design and have an image of your store, your store sign, your store logo, or some other identifying information, you can choose from a variety of other options.

    a. To add your own image, click on "Change background image" and upload your file. Remember that your image will only be seen in the columns to the right and left. Images with visual information arranged vertically along the left-hand side tend to work best.
    b. If you do not have your own image, you can select from numerous Twitter template backgrounds. Still in Settings, under the "Design" tab, you can select from a handful of backgrounds just by clicking on one.

3. *Adding personal information*: In Settings, under the Account tab, there are a variety of fields worth filling out. Here you can display your URL, add a short bio, and let people know some things about your business.

Finding People

Finding people on Twitter can be challenging. By clicking on "Find People" on the top right-hand corner of the page, you can search for accounts if you know their username, first or last name, or email. In our experience, this search tool can be unreliable and requires that you know and spell the name perfectly. If you don't get your desired result with the search tool, do not despair; the fellow Twitizen may still be out there.

If you're not looking for anyone in particular, but are searching for people involved in different businesses, try using the search bar above the trend list. For example, if you are in the restaurant business and are looking for people discussing professional-grade stoves, consider typing the brand and model into the search bar to see if anyone has mentioned that keyword in a tweet.

Understanding Twitter Lingo

Since Twitter launched in 2006, users themselves have invented special tweet conventions that add a layer of complexity to the status updates. Over time, Twitter adopted some of these conventions and integrated them into their site. Understanding these conventions is important to deciphering and creating tweets that serve different purposes.

- @reply: The @reply is by far the most commonly used special lingo on Twitter. What the @reply does is direct a tweet at a single person or a group of people. Since most people ignore @replys that don't involve them, use them sparingly. They are a terrific way to engage people and show that you care about that engagement, an important component of online customer service, but using @replys too much means your message might get ignored. To use, simply place the "@" sign before a username anywhere in the tweet, typically at the beginning:

- RT (Re-tweet): The re-tweet is an attribution method used to forward the tweets of others while giving them credit. Beginning a tweet with RT means that the tweet info belongs to someone else and you found it interesting enough to post on your own feed. If there's enough space, always mention why you thought the tweet was worth re-tweeting. To use, place the "RT" at the beginning of the tweet followed by the attribution @[username].

- DM (Direct message): The DM is a way to tweet with another person directly and privately. DM tweets are the only tweets that do not appear on your feed, and are instead filed away in a separate feed you can access by clicking "Direct Messages" on your interface. To DM someone, you must follow them, and they you. DM's are an effective way to send personal messages that may only be interesting for the recipient: To use, use the tweet with DM followed by the username.

- #hashtag: The hashtag is designed to group a tweet into a trend of similar tweets. For example, you could group a tweet about the World Series by ending the tweet with #worldseries. People can then find your tweet just be searching for the hashtag. By searching by hashtag, you can filter out all the tweets about a specific topic. Even though you can create your own, we recommend ending tweets with a common, simple hashtag. To use, end the tweet with #[hashtag], e.g., #socialmedia or #besthamburger.

Link Shortening

Including links to outside websites is a common way to add value and interest to your tweets. However, as you can already guess, links can be very long. Luckily, there are several online services that will reduce any link to 20 characters. Our favorite can be found at Bit.ly (http://bit.ly/). Bit.ly will not only shorten your link, but track how many people click on it. Keep in mind that unless you create a user account with Bit, the tracking feature will be available only when you use the same browser on the same computer.

Tips for Successful Tweeting

1. Have a consistent presence. Commit to tweeting once in the morning, once at night. Twice each is better. Because people often follow hundreds of people, fighting through the clutter requires that you be an active tweeter.

2. Vary the content of your tweets. Review the messaging recommendations in Chapter 4 to get some great ideas on different types of content you can use in your tweets.

3. Limit self-promotion. Direct self-promotion rarely works. Before tweeting, ask yourself, "Is this something I would like to hear myself?" Tweet about special events, promotions, or new products, not about how great your business is.

4. Track and measure your activities on Twitter: see Chapter 7 for more information.

5

Say Goodbye to the Yellow Pages: Strategies to Optimize Search

---

> I don't know what people use the Yellow Pages for anymore . . . other than a giant coaster.
>
> —Della Mendenhall (Gillespie Florist)

How do new customers find out about basic information about your business? In the past, you have probably used different types of traditional media to accomplish this: a television or radio spot, direct mailers, a newspaper ad, a billboard, or a display ad in the Yellow Pages. All these tactics have one thing in common: they come with a cost. Additionally, these traditional tactics just do not work as well as they used to, because people tend to use the Internet, and now their mobile phones, to find out basic information (such as your business's address, phone number, and operating hours). Many small business owners like Brad Niva (Rogue Wilderness Adventures) are eager to eliminate the paper version of the Yellow Pages and focus their efforts (and the dollars they spend in the paper version of the Yellow Pages) online.

In addition, people look to these online listings to indicate that a visit to your business is worth their time. Whether using a search engine such as Google or Bing, or a user-review site such as Yelp, people not only want to know what's out there, but also what people have to say about it, all without having to call a friend or dig out a book in a drawer. As Robbie Vitrano (Naked Pizza) has found, "our initial customers are going to be online people that understand technology and understand tools."

Therefore, if people do not easily find your business when they search for your business online, many potential customers simply will not know you exist.

A 2009 study by two research organizations, GroupM Search and comScore, showed a relationship between search marketing and social media. In particular, the study found that people who use search engines who also engage with a brand's social media are much more likely to search for that brand than people who didn't engage with social media. People involved with a brand's social media are more likely to click on search results leading to a brand's site. Overall, the study concludes that people who use search engines and social media are more engaged overall, and are more likely to act on information they find online, such as purchasing products and visiting stores (comScore, 2009).

Most small businesses already have some type of website for their business. Adam Cuppy (Dutch Bros. Coffee) sees the website as an extension of the store: a presence that is open whenever a customer wants to find information about the business. By extension, he sees that social media complements the business website, by providing an indication of the customer experience 24/7. Jillian Bisinger and Tony Zucca (Jillian Bisinger Modern Photography) see their website as being able to provide much more in-depth information about services, prices, and packages than on a typical social media site.

However, some businesses may be hesitant about creating a website due to the cost of hiring someone to develop the site, time management, or concerns that they do not have sufficient content to put on a site. (A pet store, for example, has many different products to sell. If the store does not sell those products online, the business owner may question whether there is sufficient content for the site.) One relatively simple way to get an online website up with minimal effort is to have a blog for your business. Throughout this book, we have talked about how blogs can enhance the online user experience and draw customers to your business, but they can also be complete sites for your business, complete with different pages and media. By using a platform such as WordPress or Blogger, you have a free and simple way to create and manage a site without needing any technical knowledge.

These blogging sites provide free templates that you can customize: you can select the appearance of the pages, change colors, insert or remove buttons or widgets, etc. You can even have a custom URL, and your page will be fully indexed by search engines so your blog will appear in searches related to our business. Justin Stobb (All Wheel Drive Auto) created a website for his business using a WordPress blog for their online site. By having a multiple-page blog, with different pages devoted to different aspects of the business such as "making appointments" and "parts information," the blog takes on the appearance of a traditional website.

Many retailers believe that you can replace space in the traditional Yellow Pages by utilizing free services online. Furthermore, you can optimize your website to include terms and keywords that people are likely to search. In this chapter, we will focus on resources that anyone with a computer can use, with no knowledge of Internet coding required. We will briefly discuss some advanced techniques for optimizing your website so you can better address the strengths and weaknesses of your site, either yourself or with a web designer.

How Search Works

Search engines are complex computer programs that use automated applications called "spiders" to crawl (or travel throughout) the Internet. Think of these spiders as gold prospectors, who leave camp each day to look for treasure. The only difference is that in the online spider's case, all the gold is in plain sight, waiting to be found and catalogued. Through this process, billions of spiders have indexed the web, meaning they have created a detailed map of the entire Internet that can be searched nearly instantly by engines such as Google or Bing. Of course, this map is always being redrawn as spiders discover brand new content every day. To continue the metaphor, the goal of any business should be to create as much gold to be found as possible.

According to the online research firm Net Market Share, the three most popular search engines are Google, Microsoft's Bing, and Yahoo. In 2010, Google dominated the search market, with nearly 85 percent of the market share. Yahoo! and Bing were at 6 percent and 3 percent, respectively. Fortunately, each site uses similar techniques to index to the web so you do not need to address each search engine individually in your site.

Types of Search

There are three main types of search results: organic, paid, and local.

- *Organic*: These results are the "main" search results on a search engine, and populate most of the page. You cannot pay a search engine to rank you highly in an organic search, as these search results are determined only by how relevant a search engine believes that site is to a search query. What are some of the factors affecting relevancy? Every search engine is different, but factors include:
  - How often the site is updated
  - The scope of the content (amounts of text, video, and photos)
  - Numbers of links in to your site and links out of your site
  - Keyword usage

In the case of Google, they look not only at how relevant a site's content is, but also the "authority" of the site, or how respected the site is, which is measured by a proprietary algorithm. If your website appears high in the organic, or nonpaid, search results, you can be generally assured that it will appear similarly on the other sites.

- *Paid*: Unlike organic search results, individual businesses or their marketing representatives bid on where a business will be placed in the list of results (if you are a restaurant, for example, you might want to pay to be included in "italian restaurants in LA" or "affordable pasta restaurant"). These results generally appear either before the organic results (at the top of the page), or on the side of the organic results page. Paid search results are generally denoted with a different-colored background and/or text that reads something like "sponsored links." With paid results, it is possible to buy your way to the top quickly. With organic search results, it may take months for the content of your site to be fully indexed and for your site to appear high in the results. Many businesses begin with paid search to direct traffic to their site while it climbs up the ladder of organic search results.
- *Local*: Local search results appear in a list alongside a map when a user searches a category and a geographic location, for example,

"pizza Austin Texas." These results are relatively new additions to search engines and require a business owner or representative to create an account with the search engine. Once an account has been created, when a user clicks on your business name, they will be taken to your business's profile, which may have directions, hours, specials, reviews, and maybe a link to your website if the person wants to continue further. Unlike organic results, which take time, and paid results, which cost money, local results allow businesses to appear at the top of the page quickly and for free. More on these local search opportunities later in this chapter.

Optimizing Your Site for Search Engines

Whether you have a simple informational site, or a complex e-tail site, you want to be certain that you can be found easily on search engines, and not just by individuals searching the exact name of your business. If you are a crafts store, you want to appear high in the search results, even when people use search terms like "quilting supplies in Kalamazoo" or "holiday decorations midtown Manhattan."

The process of enhancing your site specifically for search engines is called search engine optimization (SEO). While you could hire a business to optimize your site for you, most of what they do can be done with a basic knowledge of how search works, what search engines look for, how to make simple modifications to an existing websites, and of course, time. Search engines use complex algorithms to measure what information is most important on a site, so it can deliver the most relevant results for a search query. Therefore, optimizing your site must be about determining what terms people are searching related to your business and creating content that targets those terms. This is becoming more important, as people increasingly use their mobile phones to access a search engine like Google, and only three or four sites will show up on the phone screen.

Integrate Appropriate Words, Phrases, and Common Search Terms into Your Website

The first step is to determine how people find your business online—or, to put it another way, to determine what words people use when searching for what you sell. Talk to your customers, staff, and your friends and family about how they might use Google to find a business like yours. Create a list of terms and phrases that people use in everyday conversation, and avoid single words. In order to cover all your bases, make sure this list includes:

o The purpose of your website, including descriptions of what you sell

o Questions that people ask about your products or services

o What problems your product or service solves (or, to think another way, the needs your products or services meet)

o Local and geographic terms that people could use to search for you; this could include names of cities, states, zip codes, or city districts (Maxwell, 2010)

During the redesign of the site for WW Windows, an independent window installer in the Bay Area, owner Dan Bohan created this type of list; the top results were:

1. Replacement vinyl windows bay area
2. Replacement vinyl windows San Francisco
3. Replacement vinyl windows Oakland
4. Window installer bay area
5. New home windows bay area
6. Milgard windows bay area
7. Replace windows in Oakland

> 5.1 Action Idea: Keep a small pad of paper at the checkout register in your store, and have your salespeople ask customers what words they would use to search for your store on Google.

If you have a Google account, you can use the Google AdWords Keyword Tool to assess which words and phrases are the most popular for searching your business. This tool is found at the Google AdWords site: http://www.Google.com/AdWords.

Next, take your keywords and phrases and make sure you are using them throughout the site. In Dan's case, the final list had several dozen phrases, and he noticed key terms like "replacement vinyl windows" and "bay area window installer" began to emerge frequently. These terms were then used throughout the site wherever they were appropriate, whether that be in the actual content, the headers, or descriptions of the images.

For example, the content on the page was changed from:

"WW Windows is the best window installer in the Bay Area"
to:
"WW Windows is the Bay Area's best installer of replacement vinyl windows, serving San Francisco, Oakland, San Jose, and surrounding areas. We are proud to carry Milgard vinyl windows, as well as Amerimax, Cascade, Therma-tru, and Hunter Douglas."

Using the brand names that the business carried, then, meant that WW Windows would show up in searches for that brand of windows. These key search terms were used throughout the site on every page with positive results. In only eight months, the company's website went from having no presence on Google to appearing on the first page of the organic search results in an extremely crowded and competitive market. That is the power of good keyword research and integration. One thing to notice is that Dan focused on using phrases, not single words. More people search using phrases than they do with single worlds, and the more specific your phrases are, the more highly targeted the traffic will be to your site.

Jillian Bisinger and Tony Zucca (Jillian Bisinger Modern Photography) use the Google Analytics program to find out what search terms are popular: Google Analytics can provide you with a list of search terms related to your business that you can consider using. (See Chapter 6 for a discussion of Google Analytics.) Use this list very strategically: the popular search terms are probably used by many of your competitors, so consider integrating some of the less popular search terms into your site so you will come to the top during searches using those terms. Jillian integrated terms that had 500–1,000 searches and found that worked very well for them.

Do not be tempted, however, to create meaningless pages on your site full of constantly repeated search terms. This specific practice is called keyword stuffing, and it is part of a strategy called "black hat SEO." This refers to using unethical techniques that impede a visitor's online experience just to attain higher search rankings. The spiders are pro-grammed to avoid this type of blatant promotion, and so doing this may hurt your ranking. Instead, always integrate your keywords into rich content that is meaningful and informational.

Have Keywords in Your URL

URL stands for Uniform Resource Locator, and is the Internet term to describe the name of your site (the words following the http://www ...). Having keywords in your URL can help your results, which is why Jillian Bisinger and Tony Zucca (Jillian Bisinger Modern Photography) made sure the words modern photography were in their URL.

Create Keyword-Rich Content

In addition to integrating your keywords into your content, creating new and useful web pages is one of the best ways to move to the top of search results. One of the easiest ways to do this is to connect your blog to your site. We have already talked about the benefits of blogs for building your community, but using a blog provides an additional benefit for your SEO. A regularly updated blog connected to your site means that you are consistently creating new content for the spiders to index. Remember though, you have to integrate the blog into the root folder of your site. The root folder is the first or top-most directory in your site's hierarchy. It can be likened to the root of a tree—the starting point where all branches (your other folders) originate. If this sounds like a foreign language to you, you may want the help of a local web designer to connect your blog to your site.

Justin Stobb (All Wheel Drive Auto) has a goal of being seen as an expert in auto repair. By creating rich content on his site, and using keywords that he identified as those used by people looking for both auto repair and auto parts, he found that he had increased his standing in organic search. Another tactic Justin uses is repeating popular blog posts. He wrote a post one year in May about highway wind noise in Subarus, a popular complaint he hears every summer. He repeats this blog post at the start of every summer driving season.

Use the phrases on your social media sites as well. Although social media sites are not indexed as often on Google, smaller search engines do index them, and it is likely Google will catch up soon. Use one of your phrases in every posting you do on Facebook, and consider using a phrase as a hashtag on Twitter. What is a hashtag? When you write a tweet, for example, and end it with the pound sign (#) and a phrase, you have a created a hashtag, which is searchable by other Twitter users. For example, Dan (WW Windows) might post something on Twitter about a new model he carries, and use the hashtag #Milgardwindows to end the tweet.

Add Valuable Content on New Pages to Your Site

Adding pages to your site that contain the keywords and phrases you've developed will also increase the odds that your site will come up high on searches. For example, the web designer at WW Windows created a product page for every type of window the company installs. At each of these product pages, visitors can find information about the manufacturer and their most popular models. Of course, anyone can find this information on the site of the actual manufacturer, but it was the perfect opportunity to accomplish two key goals: the creation of keyword-rich pages, and the hosting all the information a customer needs to request an estimate or make a purchase. Della Mendenhall (Gillespie Florist) has different pages for different situations when one might purchase flowers, including traditional categories such as "new baby," "anniversary," and "birthday" as well as novel categories such as "for him" and "Colts" (flowers in the team colors of the NFL football team in Indianapolis, the Colts).

5.2 Action Idea: What do you feature on your website that is unique to your business? Think about creating a special page devoted to that unique feature. It will enhance your organic search results, and also will distinguish you from your competitors.

Be Linkable

Links are ways to build your authority. Links have been called the "life blood" of the World Wide Web (Rosenthal 2010), and they come in three basic varieties: incoming links, outgoing links, and internal links.

o   Incoming links are critical in establishing the value of your site and helping search engines determine what other people think your site is all about. Encourage people to link to your site. For example, if you have ever sent an email with a link to a YouTube video, you have linked YouTube. Websites that rise to the top of an organic search tend to benefit from inbound links. The best incoming links to get are links from related sites, even sites that may compete with your site for visitors, but who are motivated to link you by some unique content on your site.

o   Outgoing links help the search engines determine which neighborhood you live in and what you think your own site is about. Link to sites that are authoritative and that complement the information on your site.

o   Internal links let people navigate your website, establish the webmaster's view of page hierarchy, and reinforce how the search engines categorize your content.

As you may have guessed already, the best way to be linkable is to host great, interesting content on your site. One way to do this is to have current and unique information on your site. Your blog, then, becomes a great way to do this, and your frequent posts can draw in visitors from all over the web. These visitors might share your link with their own friends (and certainly inviting visitors to share the content is a good tactic). Make sure that the sites that link to you are credible; one tool for checking the history of a website is by using the WayBack Machine at http://www.archive.org.

Declare Your Site

You can wait for the spiders to crawl your site, or you can invite them to come visit you by declaring your site. All this means is that you're alerting the search engine that your site exists instead of waiting for the search engine to find you, and doing so can shorten the time lag between having your site indexed and appearing on the search engine results page. Below are some links to help you declare your site on the major search engines:

o   Google: http://www.google.com/addurl/

o   Yahoo! http://siteexplorer.search.yahoo.com/submit

o   Bing: http://www.bing.com/webmaster/SubmitSitePage.aspx

Use Review Sites

Mentions on user-review sites like Yelp, Insider Pages, and TripAdvisor usually appear in a search for the business itself. According to Brad Niva (Rogue Wilderness Adventures), Google uses Insider Pages as their main review source. Like Google Places, the overall rating for your business is displayed directly in the results after a standard Google search. Clearly, a negative overall rating may keep potential customers from visiting your business, so revisit Chapter 2 to make sure you are maximizing your presence on these user-review sites, particularly the ones that are used most often in your industry.

One disadvantage of using Yelp is that your business's page will not appear in search results that do not include your business's name. However, even after a categorical search like "ice cream San Jose," a link to Yelp and all the businesses in that category will appear prominently in the results.

Develop a Site Map

Providing as much information to search engines increases the amount of information that search engines use to index sites, and so can increase the chances that you will "rise to the top." A site map is simply a textual description of your website: a page that provides a summary of all the different pages in your site. If your site consists of only one page, you do not need a site map; but if you have two or more pages, a site map is a great piece of information to submit to search engines.

Most web pages feature one of two types of site maps. The first type is an HTML site map, which is a page on your website that contains a list of links to all the pages of your website. This type of site map is often organized graphically so visitors to your site can easily find what they are looking for and see the relationship between the pages on your site. An example can be found here: http://www.cafeyumm.com/sitemap.html. The content on the HTML site map will be indexed by the various search engines

The second type is an XML file that is not seen by visitors to your site, but is used by search engines to understand and index your site. It provides web spiders with information on the number and types of pages on your site, and how often those pages are updated, which is important information for search engines.

Which type is best? An HTML site map provides information to both site visitors and to web spiders, and is easy for someone with a bit of HTML experience to write. The XML site map is better if you have an older site where pages are not linked together well, or where you have archive pages that are hard to find. If your website is easy to navigate, an HTML site map is your best bet (Campbell 2010).

You can create your own site map (either HTML of XML) very easily at a website like XML Site maps (http://www.xml-sitemaps.com/). Once you create your map, submit it to various search engines to include in the indexing. For all the search engines, you will need to register as a "webmaster," but this is a fast procedure requiring a limited amount of information about your business.

- Google: http://www.google.com/webmasters/tools (this process is fast and painless)
- Yahoo: https://siteexplorer.search.yahoo.com/submit
- Bing: http://www.bing.com/webmaster

Maintaining Your Rankings

In a perfect world, once you have achieved a top ranking on Google Search, you would be able to stay there forever. Unfortunately, that is not always the case, as new sites are being introduced and more people are searching for different products and services. The easiest way to maintain your rankings is to regularly have fresh content on your website. This serves as a reminder to the online spiders that your site is active so that they will index the new content that helps to keep your site at the top of the list. Paco Miller (Tia Juana's) makes sure he updates his sites every month in order to keep content fresh.

Work with your webmaster to have a section of your website that is easy to update—in fact, so easy that you can do the updating with a few minutes of effort. Your webmaster should be able to create some type of form that will allow you to do this. Some ways you can update your site regularly include:

- *Testimonials*: Take a customer quote (perhaps from a Yelp rating), post it on your site, and change it every week. You can also use comment cards from in-store customers or quotes from emails.

- *Company news*: Update with new products and services that you offer, employee news, changes in business hours, and other information about your business.

- *Event updates*: Add special events, offers, entertainment, community events, etc.

- *Product or service of the week*: Provide in-depth information on one specific product or service.

- *Coupon or special offering of the week*: A great deal that changes every week.

- *Trade links with other vendors*: Jillian Bisinger and Tony Zucca (Jillian Bisinger Modern Photography) link to other wedding vendors on their site and receive the same consideration in return. These links can have a big influence on Google rankings.

- *Update of site maps*: Do this whenever you add new pages.

The Value of Google Places

As we mentioned earlier in the chapter, Google Places is an example of local search. By creating an account for your business, you create a portal where you can add information about your business including a map and directions, and a place where customers can submit reviews. Google Places also provides a link directly to your business website. Google Places is free and provides reports on how many impressions you received (how many times you were in a list of search results) and how many people clicked on your business's link in the list of results, along with other data. This can give you a good idea if your business is attracting attention or if people are even looking for businesses like yours online.

One company that has made the most out of their Google Places site is Gillespie Florist. Google Places was one of the first online sites that Della Mendenhall established for the business. She sees a huge value in Google Places because she can easily upload content to the listing, including pictures, videos, and links. Her listing stands out because none of the other local florists use video. They also are the only local florist that uses coupons on the Google Places site, and she has had customers mention that they selected their shop because of this benefit. Della believes that Google Places helps her company look like they are very Internet-savvy in the minds of customers, which is a great way to distinguish the florist from other area florists. Brad Niva (Rogue Wilderness Adventure) also finds Google Places to benefit his business: His location is generally listed in the top six on the map, and Brad has included the hours of operation and examples of some of the adventure trips the company offers on Google Places. Like Della, he uploads videos and photos to Google Places and sees it as a virtual "storefront on Google."

Other search engines offer listings similar to Google Places. Yahoo offers Yahoo Local (http://local.yahoo.com/), a service that offers a free basic listing. For a monthly fee, an enhanced listing will allow you to add photos and a greater level of detail. Bing offers the Bing Local Listing Center (https://ssl.bing.com/listings/ListingCenter.aspx) that allows businesses with a Windows Live ID to create a listing and chose categories to describe your business.

Geosocial Networks, or "Lo-So"

What is lo-so? It stands for location social, and represents a new trend in social networking. These networks allow smartphone users (people who have iPhones and Blackberry devices, for example) to use an application that they've downloaded to their phone "check-in" at different locations they visit every day. The applications themselves use the global-positioning chips in the smartphones to register the user's location at the business (Albright 2010).

On an average workday, someone might check in at a bagel shop for breakfast, at their workplace, at a local diner for lunch, and perhaps at a grocery store, gas station, or video store on their way home. These "check-ins" are displayed at the lo-so website and on the user's Facebook status update page and Twitter feed. Users receive points for every check-in, and the points can turn into prizes and other incentives for the users.

Most of the listings come from users visiting different venues. You may already have a presence on a lo-so network. Many networks allow you to create a listing (called "claiming your business"), and this will allow you to add details about your business. Many businesses use lo-so to replace their traditional "frequent visitor" cards; for example, a donut shop could offer a free donut after a customer "checks in" 10 different times (this would be visible on the customer's smartphone).

The most popular lo-so networks include foursquare and Gowalla. Both these networks treat the lo-so experience as a type of a game: foursquare awards digital badges to users for frequent usage of a location (such as announcing that the most frequent user is the "Mayor" of a specific location); users display these badges on their Facebook site. Gowalla provides a physical pin that users wear that identify them as participants in the Gowalla Lo-So. Additionally, some sites allow users to track where their friends are to be able to arrange for meet-ups at convenient locations.

Even if you are not familiar with these types of platforms, they are popular and growing. People use their phones as social tools: to quickly connect with others, via either a phone call or a text message. Additionally, one in four mobile subscribers who use the web on their phone at least monthly also use their device to search for local business information (Emarketer.com 2010). Even that old standby, the Yellow Pages, is looking for ways to bring the "old" yellow pages to mobile phones so that information can easily be found and then shared with others. As such, phones are natural for social networks. Foursquare, the current leader in the Lo-So world, currently has more than 1.7 million users checking in nearly 1 million times per day. Every day, about 12,000 new people join foursquare (Albright 2010).

5.3 Action Idea: Adam Cuddy (Dutch Bros. Coffee) is one of many small businesses who are intrigued with the idea of "lo-so" networks, but is hesitant to jump into this brave new world. Adam's advice is to spend some time personally using a lo-so, so you can understand the different ways your customers might use it. Then, you can determine the optimal way to use the lo-so for your company.

Is a geosocial network right for your business? Many small business owners find that they need to use a brand-new application like a lo-so for a while before they feel comfortable using it for their business. This may be a good tactic for your business. Others feel they want a more direct connection with customers via smartphones. Paco Miller (Tia Juana's) uses text messaging to connect with his customers, especially those who frequent his nightclub, in order to alert them to events at the nightclub while they are out partying. Finally, many customers are "checking in" at businesses using foursquare, and the businesses are not even aware this is happening, and so do not even think about leveraging that opportunity. Visit the sites for foursquare (http://foursquare.com) and Gowalla (http://gowalla.com) and enter your business name into the search box on the home page. You can then quickly see if your customers are using these services.

Key Chapter Insights

- Optimize your site for organic search by creating a list of phases that people use to describe your business, its services, and the benefits it creates for your customers, and integrating these key phrases throughout online content
- Creating new, useful pages will improve your ranking. Connecting your blog to your site can often accomplish this goal.
- Declare your site to the major search engines. Don't wait for them to find you.
- Encouraging customers to review your business at sites like Yelp and Inside Pages (see Chapter 2) can improve your search ranking.
- Have one section of your website that is easy for you to update. It just takes minutes for you to post some new content or images.
- Google Places is an easy-to-use way to beat the big boys when it comes to local search.

Getting Started

- If you're brand new to social media: Research search terms and make sure that these terms appear regularly on your website.
- If you're familiar with social media: Make sure your website is mentioned on all your social media sites.
- If you are ready to move to the next level: Create a site map and submit it to search engines.

Getting Started with Google Places

In an average minute, the Google search engine processes 1.4 million search requests. Google is by far the most popular search engine online, accounting for two-thirds of all search activities of Americans. Your business can appear in the list of Google's local results, a list of businesses that appear at the top of Google search results with their locations pinpointed on a map. To appear on this list, all you have to do is register your business at Google Places. Registration is free, and you can include valuable information such as photos, videos, your business hours, and a link to your website.

How Google Places Works

Google's local search results appear anytime an online user combines a search item with a geographical modifier, i.e., "pizza san jose." The results are sorted by their relevance, which is often heavily weighted by the result's proximity to your geographical location.

For some searches that do not include a geographical modifier, Google will display local results based on Google's estimation of your current location, which is based on how you access the Internet (which tends to be less accurate than a self-entered search term). Just search "pizza," and you will likely see a list of local results as well.

Setting Up Google Places

1. Visit the Google search engine (http://www.google.com) and search for your store category (such as restaurant or gas station) and the city or region where you do business.

2. Google will provide you a map with a list of local businesses in the category.

3. Click on the underlined phrase that begins with "local business results for" or the relevant link for your search.

4. Look for the name of your business on the list that comes up.

5. *If your business name is there,* click on it. You will now be able to "claim" your business through a verification process. Verification proves that you are the owner of the business and that the information provided is correct. Here's how:

   • If verifying by phone, an automated phone call will be made to the phone number listed for the business. During this call, you'll be prompted to enter the unique PIN that Google displays in your account whenever an addition or change is made to the basic business information for your listing.

- If verifying by postcard, the PIN will be sent to you within 10 business days. You will then need to log back onto Google Places and enter the PIN before your listing will appear. Please note, postcards will only be sent to the address submitted to Google Maps.

6. If your business name is not there, scroll down to the bottom of the page and click on the words "information for business owners."

- You will be taken to a signup screen to sign up for a Google account. This is free. The "Sign Up Now" link is in the upper right-hand corner.

- Once you sign in, click on "Add New Business" in the box in the upper right-hand corner.

- Fill out your business information, including your business's name, address, phone number, web page address, and a description of the business. Once you are done, click the "next" box at the bottom.

- Now you're ready to be verified. Go back to step 5 and continue with the verification process.

Tips for Google Places Success

- Once you create your listing, you can always upload videos, images, and other information to make your listing more interactive and interesting. Basically, anything that you add to your Facebook page can be added here as well.

- You can also add coupons by clicking on the coupons tab at the top of the dashboard.

- Review and update your listings on a quarterly basis in order to verify that your listings, keywords, and categories are relevant and accurate.

6

Better than the Rotary: Using Social Media to Create a Business Network

---

> I've been in a group called BNI, Business Network International, for about a year and a half now. And that's been one really great benefit for me, especially in a smaller community like this, to really help find different business contacts and also different promotions.
>
> —Brian Mason (SKP-Popcorn)

So far, we have covered the important areas of using social media to create and nurture customer communities. One overlooked strength of social media, however, is in creating business-to-business relationships. For some businesses, their presence on Facebook and Twitter will help them to create connections with other businesses. You may also wish to become part of an online social network that is devoted solely to business.

Businesses that operate in the business-to-business (B2B) arena (as opposed to business-to-consumer arena) are involved in social media, and they find it works. Almost all B2B decision makers use social media in the buying process, and two thirds of B2B marketers use some type of social media (Pick 2010). In this chapter, we will discuss the benefits of building a business network, point out some of the online networks that the business owners we spoke with engage in, and share some tips on maximizing your presence in a business network.

Why Create a Business Network?

Whether joining an established professional network or reaching out to other businesses with your social media presence on Facebook and Twitter, business owners have found numerous benefits to being part of a business network.

Sharing Information

Online networks provide a way to connect with many different types of businesses. Sometimes you will connect with other businesses in your category that may be located in other parts of the country. You can share marketing and product tips with people who are struggling with some of the same problems and challenges that you are. Sometimes you will connect with businesses in your geographic area. In this case, you can share information with other businesses about local opportunities that benefit both companies. Some other social networks are a mix of these. You can be part of a group of people with a wide variety of interests from all over the country and all over the world. This can allow you to get a new and fresh perspective on business questions.

One of the benefits of having a professional network in social media is that it allows you to learn new ways to market your business. People in your network can help you brainstorm about your product or can refer you to people in their own personal and professional networks who might want to buy what you're selling. Realtor Utah Dave Robison, for example, has a blog that is read by real estate agents across the country. He has over 100 different realtors as friends, and is happy to share information, even some of his trade secrets and tips, with them. He finds that he gets good feedback, and he believes that eventually this network can help him get referrals in the future.

Another type of information shared by a business network is information about the industry as a whole. Some small businesses, like Gillespie Florist, are fortunate to have access to industry information by being part of a large industry network (in Gillespie Florist's case, the network is Teleflora). These types of networks provide in-depth information about the floral industry. Similarly, Brad Niva (Rogue Wilderness Adventures) belongs to Rafting America, which is a network of rafting companies.

Rafting America has a centralized website which features listings of rafting outfitters across the country, and Brad participates on a pay-per-click basis: if someone searches for outfitters in Oregon and clicks on his link at the Rafting America website, Brad pays a small fee for that click. The members of Rafting America get together annually to share ideas and to network.

Many small businesses, though, may not be working in industries that have this kind of resource, or do not belong to industries that have these types of online networks already set up. In these cases, a single individual can take the place of an industry site. Trey Pitsenberger (Golden Gecko Nursery) is known as "The Blogging Nurseryman" and found his blog has become a very important website for the nursery industry. Trey believes it became an industry blog simply because it was one of the first blogs about the nursery business on the Internet. Trey also believes that few independent nurserymen actually blog, and so his blog gives them a chance to comment on industry happenings. These nurserymen also realize that Trey's blog is read by suppliers, and so the independents know their thoughts are being heard by the right audience.

6.1 Action Idea: If you don't currently use the Internet to learn about your industry, take a few moments and set up a Google Alerts for industry news. Examples of phrases you can use are "restaurant industry news," "retail jewelry trends," or "pet shop marketing." Then you'll have access to industry information you can share with your business community.

If you are a business that produces its own line or services or products, you should think about sharing and posting images of your work. It's great to be on the cutting edge of something fresh and new, but remember to think before you post about items that belong to your customers. If you have created say, a sign, for a local business, you will want to ask permission to post photos on Facebook or elsewhere. You never know how people will want to manage the exposure of certain things. Erica Leaf (Imagine Graphics) explained the challenge this way:

> In our business we create custom graphics for a variety of business clients. And one thing that's interesting to other people is what we're

making, who's getting a new sign, who's getting their vehicle wrap, what does it look like—they want to be the first one to see this sort of new thing or to know that there's a new restaurant and their sign is going up or something. So that is one thing we like to be able to tweet about, is a current project that's just in the works or being completed. But we have a policy to make sure to ask permission of clients.

Generating Leads

Business relationships online can generate much more than a great knowledge base. For some businesses, they can generate significant sales leads. For example, Brian Mason (SKP-Popcorn) connected with a caterer at an online business network. After getting to know Brian and his popcorn products, the caterer started recommending SKP popcorn for wedding favors to her customers. Brian remembers one wedding where the theme was the Stanley Cup, and SKP-Popcorn provided red and green popcorn for wedding favors.

> 6.2 Action Idea: Make a list of different complementary businesses to your business, and focus on these types of businesses to build your network. A florist, for example, could have a list containing photographers, bakeries, limo services, reception halls, and printers. A pet store could have a list containing animal shelters, pet sitters, dog trainers, and vets.

Brian recalls that "colors are very important to brides and adding, so . . . creating different colors or flavors really helps . . . to do something special and different."

Developing Cross Promotions

Lisa Hartwick (Hartwick's Kitchen Store) found that her presence on Twitter attracted the attention of other local business owners. Once these owners began following her, she repaid the favor and followed them. She makes a point of reading their posts, and has followed up on other busineses' posts on Twitter to develop joint and cross promotions. For example, King Estate Winery is located about 30 miles outside of the city where Hartwick's is located. The marketing director at King Estate tweeted that he was looking for a site to hold a wine tasting, and Hartwick immediately responded by inviting him to hold the tasting at her store. She has plans to reach out to small, specialty food producers in the area and invite them to hold a food tasting at her store.

Finding Trusted Service Providers

Finding some to help you with your business—an accountant, a cleaning service, a landscaper—is always a challenge. You could use Google to search for companies, but all you may find is that company's website, which not provide a level of information you are confident in. For example, say you own a small restaurant. Business has been great, and now you are ready to expand. You know you need an ad agency to promote the launch of your new location. Using your network, you can easily locate any connections who have experience or knowledge in this area and tap into their expertise. If they are not able to help, it is likely someone in their personal network can. In a short amount of time, you could have a list of possible agencies that have been endorsed by those that you trust and respect, or their friends.

Recruiting New Employees

Your customers and their friends use social media, and some of these people might be looking for a job. Lisa Hartwick (Hartwick's Kitchen Store) has successfully used social media to recruit new employees. Specifically, she believes Twitter found the best employees for her company, and has hired salespeople and a store manager via Twitter. She is so impressed with Twitter as a recruitment vehicle that she has stopped all other media, including online job sites and the local newspaper classified section. She believes this works because her followers on Twitter see the message and then re-tweet it to people they know who are looking for a job. In fact, none of her new employees were followers of Hartwick's Kitchen Store before they were hired; they were all referred by followers.

One huge benefit for businesses is that recruiting in this way compresses the process so new employees can be hired fairly quickly. Lisa reported receiving resumes via email the same day that the first tweet appeared. Utah Dave Robison (Realtor) has also found that his business network that reads his blog posts and his Facebook posts can also be a good source of potential new employees. He has hired several people who were referred to him by followers on Facebook. He also sees the value of using Facebook to research employees to get a quick idea as to whether they would be a good fit for the company.

Business Network Opportunities

The business owners we spoke with belonged to a number of different online business networks: some were free, some required a membership fee, and some had other types of limitations involved. Some exist solely online, and others encourage face-to-face interaction. Several of the top business networks are provided here.

LinkedIn (http://www.linkedin.com)

LinkedIn is a social media network for entrepreneurs and professionals that gives people the opportunity to build a professional network of "connections." This can help businesspeople locate services, discover top talent, or promote your business. A basic LinkedIn membership is free, and all interactions take place online.

Like Facebook, though, LinkedIn allows businesspeople to fully customize your profile into a dynamic resume, complete with personal information like past employment, education, and recommendations from those in your network. In addition, you can easily create a company page that can be another social media outpost for potential customers to learn more about your business and services.

Recently, LinkedIn released a bevy of new features to help members collaborate, organize, and stay updated with their connections. These tools can be used to share files, host discussions, plan meetings, and synchronize calendars, giving the site benefit beyond just networking.

LinkedIn's two greatest strengths are first, the price, and second, the quality of its membership base. The basic membership in LinkedIn is free, and you get access to all types of businesspeople. The company often touts the fact that executives from every Fortune 500 company are members, but the demographics of LinkedIn's 55 million other users are just as impressive, particularly if you want to be part of a network of highly educated, successful professionals.

Biznik (http://www.biznik.com)

Biznik is another free membership site that includes both an online interaction aspect with "in-person" meetups. Biznik networks are not national like LinkedIn, but rather based around cities. There are hundreds of Biznik networks, and it is likely that you'll find one in or near your current city. Biznik encourages the sharing of ideas to help small businesses grow. It is also a simple way to find local service providers: if you need a freelance web designer or a PR professional, Biznik profiles give you an easy to search interface to find them.

BNI: Business Network International (http://www.bni.com)

A much more formal business network is Business Network International, known by its members as BNI. BNI began in the pre-Internet area in 1985, and originally started with small, location-based groups of individual businesspeople who came together regularly in person to share ideas and to network. There is an annual cost to belong to BNI; in 2010, the cost was $295 per year. Today, BNI has also moved online, but most of the basic principles remain the same.

These small (20 or so people) groups of individuals are called chapters, and each chapter allows only one individual per professional specialty to belong. The chapters allow members to share ways to improve their business and to network with other businesses. Businesspeople get business when their expertise is known and others reach a comfort level with them. BNI provides a forum that allows members to meet other business peers who need to know effective and efficient businesspeople. In 2009, members of BNI passed 6.2 million referrals that generated over $2.6 billion worth of business for each other. BNI has local chapters of businesspeople who also meet online.

Mastermind (http://www.mastermindgroups.org)

Mastermind groups offer a combination of masterminding, peer brainstorming, education, accountability and support in a group setting (either in person or online) The concept of the "mastermind alliance" was formally introduced by Napoleon Hill in his timeless classic *Think and Grow*

Rich, though mastermind groups have been around since the beginning of time. Mastermind groups tend to be smaller than BNI groups.

In a Mastermind group, the agenda belongs to the group, and each person's participation and commitment is key. The focus is less on lead generation (as in BNI) and more on gaining feedback on ideas along with brainstorming and accountability. Many mastermind groups are established under the auspices of the Napoleon Hill Foundation (http:// www.naphill.org) and even more groups are formed that are unrelated to the foundation but follow the principles that Hill outlined. The cost for the Napoleon Hill Foundation online group (in 2010) is $49.95.

EO Entrepreneurs Organization

Like BNI and Mastermind, Entrepreneur's Organization (known as EO) consists of networks of individuals who meet either in person or online in a forum to solve business challenges. Members are also able to receive their own personal mentor, and online educational programs are also available. Membership in EO is $1,400 per year.

Making the Most of Your B2B Presence

If you're like most small retailers, you'll probably be considering joining at least one of these online networks. Most likely, you'll start with one of the free networks to see whether the time commitment pays back with the quality of ideas you receive. Here are some ideas to maximize your presence in some of these organizations.

Create a Personal Account with a Great Profile

For many online business communities, your profile will be the first thing that others see. In order to have a strong profile, consider including URLs to your business site as well as to your other social media sites. Use the same keywords that you use in SEO in your profile. Think about including a picture of yourself: people tend to connect more with individuals representing a company in this type of venue. Put your face to your business brand.

LinkedIn, for example, has numerous categories where you can share information about yourself. The benefit to taking a few moments and

6.3 Action Idea: Check out the profiles of several different businesses in your area: both competitors and other businesses in your local area. What types of information do they feature on their LinkedIn profile? See what types of information you have positive reactions to, and integrate that information into your own LinkedIn profile.

filling these out is that current and former colleagues and classmates can easily find you. Even if someone was not in your graduating class, a shared school experience often creates an instant bond that can grow your network (Vermeirin 2010). The same thing goes for listing professional groups and associations: you may connect with people who do not attend your Rotary club, for example, but you still share the Rotary in common, and this helps to create a bond.

Make sure that your profile is consistent with your other brand messages, because your profile in the social media space is a marketing opportunity.

See if the Network You're Using Has a Synching Feature

On LinkedIn, for example, you can synchronize your business blog posts to your profile with tools provided by the site, such as Blog Link or Word-Press LinkedIn Application. In order to expand your network, your marketing efforts on business-oriented sites should be promoted in other channels. Include a link to your profile on your website, Facebook site, and blog. Also, think about including it in email signatures and perhaps even on your business cards. Be sure to optimize your profile for important and relevant keywords as discussed above, and allow enough of your profile to be public so search engines can rank that content accordingly.

Build a Network of Contacts

It is likely that you already know some people on the network, either customers or other local businesspeople. Reach out to the people you know to join your network. For those people with whom you have a solid relationship, ask them to write recommendations for your company, which will appear in your profile. In return, you should offer to write a recommendation for their company.

Another way to build your network is to share connections with the people in your network. One of the best things about LinkedIn is the Shared Connections feature, which allows you to find people—like potential clients—and then see what connections you have in common. In addition, building up a strong LinkedIn network and being willing to introduce others that you know and trust to each other can also increase what opportunities you can get in the future.

Finally, think about creating contacts within your own industry. Jillian Bisinger and Tony Zucca (Jillian Bisinger Modern Photography) make sure that they follow the top photographers in the wedding industry on a variety of social networks. They also invite those photographers to follow them. This also allows Jillian and Tony to have insight into how the top people in their field use social media. They try to emulate the practices of their competitors. Another value of having a network in your own field is referrals. This is valuable in the photography industry: if Jillian and Tony are contacted by a bride-to-be and they are already booked for the wedding date, they can refer the bride-to-be to another photographer. It is likely that the other photographer will return the favor. They have also found that other photographers are helpful in answering questions about the business of photography itself. Jillian and Tony use their industry network in another way, too. When they attend photography industry events and conferences, they often have many choices for seminars and social events. They use Twitter to search for the names of specific events to see who else is attending them, and make their choices by attending the events that industry leaders are also attending.

Ask Questions, but Give Answers, Too

Think of your business network efforts as you do your customer social media efforts: remember that the more the effort, activity, and interaction, the better the results. Be sure not to be the person who is just asking questions to improve your business: be sure you do your best to help others on the network. This is the only way a business network thrives.

LinkedIn, for example, provides a Question and Answer function where you can participate in answering others' questions and asking your own. It's a great way to figure out, for example, where the best place to go for short-term capital financing is or even a book list for entrepreneurs. No matter how technical or obscure the question is, there is usually someone with the knowledge to answer it. Posting an answer to a question is also a great way to establish yourself as an expert in a field and to gain useful connections. On Biznik, the "BizTalk" section of the forums is devoted solely to user questions and responses. These are great opportunities to engage with other business owners and offer feedback and solutions.

Seed Discussions

Asking questions and giving answers is one type of interaction that happens in business networks. Another type is brainstorming discussions, which can cover broad topics and can be of interest to different types of businesses. For example, you could start a discussion on "someone's dream employee" or "If you had 100 more square feet in your store, what would you do?" These can be very interesting and engaging discussions for all kinds of group members. You will have access to a wide range of points of view that could lead to interesting ideas for your business.

Promote Other Businesses and Local Events

Use your social media to promote other businesses to your followers. Also promote local events to your followers. Be sure that you use the "@" symbol to name the business, and use their Facebook or Twitter names when you do. That will link the business or event to your business. This accomplishes several things. Local businesses will see you as both a valuable partner and a good member of the community. This certainly can lead to both positive word of mouth and referrals. Community event organizers will also appreciate the support and will likely thank you in their social networks, which will also attract other businesses and potential customers.

The Hotel Lucia in Portland, for example, links to restaurants in the area after people from the hotel visit the restaurant and have a good experience. It also helps the hotel to make good recommendations about restaurants to their patrons, and it is likely the restaurants will recommend the hotel as well.

Once You Get Involved, Stay Involved

Like your social media presence that reaches out to your customers, you need to be involved in social media on a regular basis. Social media will not generate instant results, and it takes time to develop business relationships, whether on LinkedIn, via your blog, or on Twitter. Maintaining your commitment to social media is key. Frequently update your profile with the LinkedIn status feature, much like Facebook status updates.

Key Chapter Insights

- Many B2B decision makers use social media in their buying process, so there is real value to reaching out to this customer base.
- Benefits to B2B networks include lead generation and shared knowledge about the industry, marketing, and social media.
- Networking can produce cross promotions with complementary businesses that enhance exposure and generate customers as well as build a consumer network.
- Business networks can provide a big assist in recruiting new employees, as prospects can demonstrate interest in your business by following it regularly.
- Consider joining a few business networks and test the value of each to determine where to concentrate your time.
- Maximize your potential value by creating a detailed personal profile wherever possible. More information provides for more qualified interactions.
- Look for synching features on networks to optimize the exposure of your posting information.
- Ask contacts to write recommendations that potential clients can see.
- Interact with your network. Ask questions and provide responses. Pose topics on your networks to "seed" discussions.
- Promote other business partners through your other social networking activities.

Getting Started

- If you're brand new to social media: Set up your account and build your profile on LinkedIn.

- If you're familiar with social media: Investigate some of the groups and services provided via LinkedIn, and start building your network in that environment.

- If you're ready to move to the next level: Set up your own group on LinkedIn, or look into joining another online social network.

Getting Started with LinkedIn

LinkedIn is a great resource to help you build a professional network. As of March 2011, over 90 million people from around the world have a profile on LinkedIn: these include executives from all Fortune 500 companies as well as small business owners like you. LinkedIn differs from the more colloquial styles of Facebook and Twitter, and we recommend you spend a few minutes once you've registered for the site visiting other profiles to see the type of information they offer.

Create Your Profile

1.   Visit http://www.linkedin.com/ and complete the short registration form.

2.   Describe your employment situation. You can use the drop-down menu right of "I am currently:" to select the description that best fits you. Click on "Continue."

3.   Using your list of email contacts, LinkedIn can check whether any of your contacts are also LinkedIn members. We recommend this option if you have a personal relationship with most of your email contact list. You can always choose later to whom to send a connection request.

4.   Access the email that LinkedIn will send to your email inbox and click the link to verify your account. You should be automatically redirected back to the LinkedIn website, where you should click "Confirm."

5.   After signing in, you can manually enter the email address of people you already know and wish to connect with. If you are not ready to do this yet, click "Skip this step."

6.   Congratulations! You have taken the first steps to create your profile. You can view it by clicking "Profile" in the top menu. Aside from the basic information you entered when you signed up, your profile will be blank. Read more in Chapter 6 about enhancing your profile in order to create a strong and compelling picture of you and your store. Then move to the next step.

Customize Your Profile

1.   LinkedIn makes it easy to customize your profile. Hover over the "Profile" button in the top navigation and select "Edit your profile" from the dropdown menu.

2.   In the middle of the right-hand column, you'll see a box with the title "Profile Completion Tips." Here you can see all the details LinkedIn deems essential. It will help you keep track of what you need to do.

3. To add information about yourself, just click the links next to the green addition signs. Not all of these areas may apply to you, but do take some time to think about each section, even if you end up leaving it blank.

4. As you add information, a status bar located in the right-hand column will track your progress. When "Profile Completeness" reaches 100 percent, you have met or exceeded all of LinkedIn's expectations for a vibrant personal page.

Create a Company Page

A company page, like a website or a Facebook "Official" page, is another online outpost for your business. However, the information and description you choose to include should be targeted toward other professionals.

1. Hover over the "More" button in the top navigation. A drop-down menu should appear; click on "Companies."

2. On the next page, click "Add a company" on the right-hand side. If you are already an employee of a company that has a page on LinkedIn, the "Add a company" button will be in small type above your company name.

3. Just as with your profile, there are a variety of opportunities to customize the page. Keep in mind, though, that unless your business focuses specifically on B2B services or products, it is unlikely many consumers will visit this page. Therefore, tailor the information to other businesses or individuals you may want to partner with.

Add LinkedIn Apps and Features

LinkedIn and third-party developers offer "apps" (short for applications) that can spice up your profile, make networking easier, or organize your schedule. Luckily, adding and customizing these are both simple to do.

To add an app, hover your cursor over "More" in the top navigation and select "Application Directory" from the drop-down menu. There are currently 13 applications, and you can explore those that may be best suited to you. You can add or delete applications at any time, and yes, they are free. Three apps we like are:

- Events—allows you to post your schedule and compare it to those of your connections.

- WordPress—imports your WordPress blog to your LinkedIn profile page. The same can be done for Twitter using "Tweets."

- Company Buzz—allows you to track what LinkedIn members are talking about according to keyword.

Click on the application link for a more thorough description or to add it. On the next page, just click "Add an application" in the bottom right-hand corner.

Building Connections

The best way to build connections on LinkedIn is to invite the ones you already have in real life to the site. This may take a bit of searching at the LinkedIn site, but once you build your network, you'll never need that clunky Rolodex again. Additionally, you'll have up-to-date information about where your connections are working, so you'll be able to find them even if they change jobs. Remember, LinkedIn suggests that you have a personal relationship with a member outside the site before initiating direct contact. This means that LinkedIn prefers that you not approach people that might not know you already: it is LinkedIn's way of helping users not get spammed constantly.

Join Some Groups

LinkedIn groups are circles of people, sometimes thousands of them, united by their interest or membership in a particular organization. On the site, there are alumni groups, corporate groups, and groups just interested in a particular topic.

Groups matter because they make it easy to find like-minded professionals (and these individuals can then become your connections). There are discussion boards where you can start a dialogue with anyone, any day of the week, and maybe make a connection out of it.

To access the Group Directory, click on "Groups" in the top navigation. Here you can browse through the featured groups or search through groups by keyword or category.

Check Out "LinkedIn Answers"

LinkedIn Answers is a section of LinkedIn that gives you the ability to ask the LinkedIn community a question about anything (almost all are business related, and some can be very technical) and get a response from another member. Or you can become an expert in the field by answering a question yourself.

- To access Answers, hover your cursor over "More" in the top navigation and select "Answers" from the drop-down menu.
- You can ask or answer a question using the chat box, or you can search for questions you may be interested in by using the "Advanced Answers Search."

Locating those who are asking the right questions or those you can help, whether as a business or an individual, is a great way to begin building connections. If you are a frequent answerer of questions, you will likely be contacted by other LinkedIn members inquiring about your expertise and services.

Search for Employees

Finding employees for spec jobs or even full-time employment is a snap using LinkedIn.

- To do so, use the top right search bar.
- With the option bar set to "People," search the skill you are seeking. In our example, we used "web developer." The results page will be populated with a variety of results located across the country. We would like to narrow these results to one geographic area.
- To do so, use the "Filter by" box on the left side to enter a geographic location. Your search results will then be reduced to a manageable list that you can sort through. Be sure to investigate people's profiles before making contact. View their profile page, check their experience, certify their references (if they have any), and visit their web page. Taking these steps will ensure you've found the best people to reach out to and possibly interview.
- Using the left-hand column, you can always refine search results further and further. However, as you apply more filters, the actual number of results will diminish.

Post a Job

To post a job, hover your cursor over the "Jobs" button and click "Post a job" on the drop-down menu. Fill out the required information, and your job will be posted. LinkedIn offers a variety of ways to advertise your job for a set fee;

however, this may not be suited to your posting and is not required to get a response.

Tips for Successful Participation on LinkedIn

1. Have a clear and informational profile.

2. Review the messaging recommendations in Chapter 6 to get some great ideas on different types of content you can use on LinkedIn.

3. Limit self-promotion. Direct self-promotion rarely works. Spend more time helping others than helping yourself.

7

Media Metrics: Measuring the Effects of Social Media

We started seeing a trend on Twitter where people would talk about us, not to us, but amongst themselves about us. When we search it, we see there's this chatter that we didn't initiate, we see that there's chatter on Facebook, "Hey, let's have my after 30th birthday dinner at Qoola, and everybody's meeting at Qoola," things like that, that we didn't have any part of. So there's no real tangible way to measure your ROI on one tweet.

—Jesse Yu (Qoola)

Mitch Betts, in a poll reported at the MarketingProfs website, outlined the top barriers to measuring social media return on investment (ROI). He reported that many marketers believed that measuring the ROI of social media campaigns is important, but 70 percent of respondents confessed that their companies are not doing enough to actually measure the results. The companies cited the following factors as the biggest barriers:

- Lack of dedicated resources to do the measurement and analysis: 30 percent
- Don't know what to measure: 25 percent
- Social media isn't primarily about ROI: 20 percent
- Lack of tools: 14 percent

The Measurement Challenge

Businesses want to be able to measure the impact of social media, but often do not know where to start: simply deciding what to measure. Because people join social network sites to be social, you will rarely find a direct connection between their social media activity and something you can monetize, like purchases. Measuring your return on your investment of your social media activity can be a challenge. Unfortunately, many of these challenges keep small businesses from implementing measurement systems, which eventually limits the effectiveness of any marketing program.

One challenge specific to social media is data availability: depending on the social network site, you may be able to access data directly through the site, or you may have to use other online tools as aids. For example, Facebook Insights measures a series of metrics all within the Facebook site. Twitter, on the other hand, lacks that functionality and you will have to use third-party tools such as TweetBeep or Twitterboard. The second challenge is the nature of changes over time: looking at measurements for one day or one week is not going to give you the insights you need to draw conclusions. Examining changes over time is more valuable, but you may run into the first challenge: the availability of the data to measure changes over time. To start, go back to Chapter 1 and think about your own goals for your social media presence (think especially about that "m" in the SMART mnemonic). For measurements to be effective, they must line up with the measurable objectives that you have already set. Did you plan to get people following you, to get them to interact with you, to get them to talk to their friends about you? Was it to have your business mentioned in a variety of media? Was it to increase the amount of positive mentions about your business? Whatever that initial goal was, that should be the basis where you begin your measurement.

Effective measurement is rarely based on one measure alone. Usually a combination of measures is the best indication of your progress toward your goals and objectives. Effective measurement can utilize either quantitative and qualitative measurements. Quantitative measurements are those measurements that are counted or expressed numerically. Quantitative data can be represented visually in graphs and charts. Qualitative research is a much more subjective form of research, in which the researcher determines what data is important and what isn't. Often the data presented from qualitative research will be much less concrete than pure numbers as data. Instead, qualitative research may yield stories, or pictures, or descriptions of feelings and emotions

As a next step, determine your benchmark. Two types of benchmarks are important to small businesses. The first type of benchmark is the performance of your business over time. You may wish to measure and monitor every week, or every month. As you collect your data, you will be able to compare to previous time periods to see how you have progressed and where you need to place more efforts. The second type of benchmark is your competition. In this chapter, we have provided some guidelines for some measures based on available industry data. In Chapter 8, we provide more information on how to do a social media audit, which will provide you with a good idea of how your competitors are performing in social media. This chapter will allow you to develop benchmarks that are much more personalized for your business. Regardless, benchmarks are important. Tracking these measures regularly provides you with more information about what to focus on in your own social media efforts.

Types of Measurement

There are many different types of measurements that can be tracked, and they fall into four categories:

- Followers—numbers of people who follow you and who interact on your social media presence
- Engagement—numbers and quality of interactions on your social media site
- Mentions—quality and quantity of content that users share with others
- Conversions—sales directly attributable to a social media message

You might notice that these four categories fall into a hierarchy. Followers are the basic measure, and everyone wants to be growing their base of followers consistently. While that is a good start, it is important not to stop there. Followers are great, but followers that actively talk to you via social media are even better. This period of talking to you is the point we define as engagement. It is the first step in building an actual relationship with a customer or potential customers. Additionally, at the engagement level we see customers talking among themselves at your social media sites. These types of interactions will help to strengthen your community.

Once you have built this relationship, it is likely that your followers will begin to talk about your business in other venues: on ratings sites, on their own Twitter feeds and Facebook walls, and in blogs. It is terrific when your community talks to each other, but it is even better when the community starts to share great things about your business with people who are not in your community; that's the key to word of mouth. That's the point when the word-of-mouth process really starts to take off. This is the "mentions" level in the hierarchy. The last category, as you see, is the action category: conversions of messages to sales. Frankly, conversions will be hardest to track, simply because it is often difficult to make the direct link between the message and the sale (that is, beyond a "Twitter-only" discount, for example).

> 7.1 Action Idea: Use the hierarchy to set goals for your business. For example, check out how many followers you have and then set a goal for the next month to increase those followers by, for example, 20 percent.

Facebook Metrics

Facebook provides several tools that page owners and administrators can access easily. These tools provide a baseline of quantitative data that you can use to track your visitors' activities. Additionally, you can develop some quantitative and qualitative metrics on your own that can help you get a better picture of what is happening on your Facebook page. Page owners/administrators have access to an "insights" box on the left-hand column of your page. Adam Wallace (Roger Smith Hotel) finds these measurements are important in that they provide top-line data regarding activity on your page, presented in the form of graphs.

- The "users" graph displays the total number of people who "like" your page (a follower measure) as well as the number of people who are daily active users of your page. This data includes:

- ○ Daily active users—by day, the number of people who visit your page. You can track and see which days of the week are the most popular, correlating this information to specific posts. This can indicate the types of posts that attract the most visitors.

- ○ By day, the number of people who "dislike" your page. This could be a reaction to specific content, a reaction to some in-person interaction at your business, or the result of an individual "culling" their Facebook lists. If you get one or two dislikes a week, it should not be a concern. One day that generates five or more dislikes should lead you to investigate what might have happened. Specifically, did you post something that upset people or turned them off to your business?

- ○ A graph of demographics, which shows a breakdown of your fans by age, gender, and country of origin (a follower measure).

- ○ The activity measure, which shows in addition to visiting the page, what other types of activities visitors engaged in. These could include downloading images, watching videos, and listening to podcasts (an engagement measure).

- The interactions graph is an engagement measure. Most people will want to keep a steady amount of interactions going on at the page, with interactions increasing when important things are announced on the page. The interactions measured in the Insight box include:

  - ○ Total Interactions on the page (the total number of wall posts and comments to wall posts on the page)

  - ○ Total comments on the page (the total number of responses to your wall posts)

  - ○ Total wall posts on the page (the number of different posts made by you, and others, to your wall)

In addition to these measurements, you can track other activities on your own. These include:

- Follower measures
  - ○ *Number of page followers*: As often as you wish, you can track the number of people who follow—or like—your page. On Facebook, this information is on the left-hand column, about halfway down

the page. Most small businesses we spoke with had a goal of having 1,000 followers; this number tended to be based on what "other" businesses had and what they thought was possible. You can use competitive information (see Chapter 8) to refine this number.

> **7.2. Action Idea:** One way *not* to build a good network is to purchase followers from companies that sell them. Purchasing followers (for as little as 10 cents each on Facebook) gives the illusion your business is popular, but it is highly unlikely these followers will become active participants on your site. Instead, take the money you might spend on followers and offer incentives to your current followers. They will spread the word and likely attract more followers to your site. You will create happy customers, too.

o *Increase in followers*: Most businesses want to be consistently increasing the total number of people following them. As a rule of thumb, increasing your total followers by 4 percent every month is in line with average Facebook growth (M+R Strategic Services 2010). Some days will be more, some days will be less, but this type of increase shows a conservative and consistent growth.

o *Follower's activities*: In addition to a raw count of followers, you can track your friends/fans daily and correlate the data to other activities that you are doing to attract people to your page. For example, if you send out an email message inviting people to your page, you can see if your numbers increase after the email goes up.

• Engagement measures

o *Number of active versus passive followers*: How many of your followers are actively engaged on your page—posting content, asking questions, even indicating that they like a certain post? The more engaged your followers are, the more likely they are to spread the word about your business. Your goal should be to constantly increase these followers. Your goal should be to have about 2.5 percent of your fans interact each week on your site (M+R Strategy Services 2010) and have 10 percent of your followers becoming regular active participants on your social media site.

○ *Number of comments about brand or product*: You want to track the response to the actual posts you make on your page. An average business posts about six times per week. Your goal should be to achieve a certain level of engagement with every post. If 2.5 percent of your fans should be interacting every week, then about 0.4 percent of your fans should reply to every post. If you have 1,000 fans, for example, then 4 people should respond to every post. Topics that generate comments are the types of posts you should continue doing. If a topic generates no comments, reduce your use of that type of post in the future.

○ *Quality of comments on the brand page*: Some comments to your posts will be short and sweet: "I agree!" or "I love your store!" While these are great, having followers write longer and more thoughtful posts will do more to build your brand. Track whether you are getting more "higher-quality" comments as time goes on by counting the number of words in an average post. Higher quality posts have more words and sentences.

• Mention measures

○ Track the number of times a follower uses the @ symbol to talk about your business. These comments will appear to other people in your followers' network, and may encourage others to follow you and, hopefully, engage in discussions and talk to others about your business.

• Conversation measures

○ If you offer a "Facebook-only" deal, track how many people take advantage of the deal.

○ While it might not be an overwhelming number, be sure you track how many leads come from Facebook. Utah Dave Robison (Realtor) found that in his first three or four months using Facebook, he had five deals that came out of relationships built at the social network site.

Twitter Metrics

Twitter does not provide the "Insights" that Facebook does, but it is fairly simple to keep track of some top-line data of your Twitter users.

- Follower measures
  - *Number of followers*: How many people are following you, and how is that growing over time? Your goal should be 1,000 followers (Authority Domains 2010), and your Twitter following should be growing at about 9 percent per month (M+R Strategy Services 2010).
  - *Speed of growth*: Track when the followers started following you (Twitter should send you an email detailing this information). Does the growth in followers come in spurts, maybe in response to the release of new information, or is the growth steady? Steady growth can mean a brand with strong, consistent awareness. Growth spurts can mean that people started following you based on their interest in one specific post that may or may not be characteristic of your other tweets. For example, if you re-tweeted some celebrity gossip, you may get many new followers that are much more interested in that celebrity than they are in your business.
- Engagement measures
  - *Number of questions or comments*: Track the number of times people directly contact you with a question or comment.
  - *Are you listed?* Twitter users can organize the people they follow into lists. These offer a way to group together the people one follows on Twitter so the user can get an overview of what they're up to: one list might be for a user's family members, another for work colleagues, another for businesses or an industry they follow. While lists do not necessarily suggest that you are being closely followed, they do show that someone is interested enough in you to segment your tweets into a group with like-minded tweeters. To see how many lists you are part of, click the "lists" link in the upper right-hand corner of your Twitter home page. While there is no simple way to increase the likelihood that someone will add you to a list, providing consistent and interesting tweets may help that to happen.

> 7.3. Action Idea: If you haven't done so, set up searches on Google Alerts and Social Mention (see Chapter 2 for more information).

- Mention measures

  ○ *Re-tweets*: On average, a business tweets about 4.5 times per day. Measure how often and what types of messages that you post on Twitter are re-tweeted. People re-tweet messages that interest them, and that they think will interest others. To measure this, look at the right-hand side of your Twitter home page and click on the "Re-tweet" link. Click on the tab that says "your tweets, re-tweeted" and you can get an idea of your most popular tweets.

    > 7.4 Action Idea: Set a goal that at least three of your tweets will be re-tweeted each month. Track to see what types of tweets generate re-tweets, and work those types of tweets into your regular tweeting plan.

    For some businesses, having every third tweet re-tweeted is the norm. Somer Deck (Fifth Street Public Market) uses this metric to track her re-tweets, and watches for the types of tweets that are re-tweeted. For other businesses, followers will not re-tweet messages often, but like Fifth Street Public Market, what is most important to notice is what types of topics get the most re-tweets. These are the types of messages that are likely to be resonating with many customers, and they give you an idea of what topics to focus on in future tweets.

  ○ *Your business mentions*: While on your Twitter home page, click on the link with your username preceded by the "@" symbol; on our page, it would be @smlbizsmarts. This shows you all the times people tweet about your brand. Jesse Yu (Qoola) uses this tactic often. He often sees conversations about his store not initiated by the store: people tweeting things like "Hey, let's have my after 30th birthday dinner at Qoola" and "Everybody's meeting at Qoola before the movie."

- Conversion measures

  ○ *Response to special offers*: Robbie Vitrano (Naked Pizza) sends out "special offers" via Twitter, and instructs his staff to count the number of people mentioning Twitter. Somer Deck (Fifth Street Public Market) uses coupons to attract visitors to the marketplace, and these coupons are offered primarily via Twitter. Somer has found that their customers respond to this tactic. In addition, Somer uses coupon-tracking codes so that she can see how quickly the customer redeemed the coupon and where they used it. Additionally, Somer finds that people re-tweet these offers, so the coupon spreads virally, which should be the goal of any promotion.

○ *Leads*: Track sales from people who mention they follow you on Twitter. Erica Leaf (Imagine Graphics) found that the printing company has received several jobs from her tweets, and the jobs were significant in size.

Five additional tools can be accessed to help you track your Twitter messages and followers.

- Bit.ly (http://bit.ly/): this service allows users to take a long URL and shorten it. It is used often by Twitter users who post links to other sites in their tweets: having a short URL allows more characters for the actual tweet. In addition, Bit.ly tracks how your shared links are performing. You will get click data, referrer information, location graphs, and related conversations. The service is one good way to know what types of tweets are popular and instigate the most conversations.

- TweetBeep (http://www.tweetbeep.com): TweetBeep is a tool that allows you to keep track of conversations that mention you, your products, and your company. You can even keep track of who's tweeting about your website or blog, even if they use a shortened URL (like bit.ly or tinyurl.com). This can be especially useful to track when people are re-tweeting your tweets.

- Qwitter (http://www.useqwitter.com): Qwitter is a tool that emails you when somebody stops following you on Twitter—and tells you the last tweet they read. The service aims to give you an idea of what type of content may have turned off a former follower. In addition, you may wish to send the person a personalized message inviting them to continue following you.

- TweetMeme (http://tweetmeme.com/): If you have a blog for your business, you can use the TweetMeme re-tweet buttons to encourage visitors to tweet your blog posts on Twitter. TweetMeme then allows you to track how your blog posts were shared via re-tweets and bit.ly analytics.

- HootSuite is a third-party application that allows you to tweet from a smartphone as well as from a computer. HootSuite now includes Google Analytics (see below) in its dashboard, allowing instant access to a range of information.

Blog Metrics

Many website owners and bloggers chose to use a free product called Google Analytics (http://www.google.com/analytics) to track activities on blogs and websites. Once you set up an account with Google Analytics, you are provided with a short piece of software code that you can easily add to the code of your website and/or blog.

Google Analytics tracks daily activity at your website or blog and then presents that information in an easy-to-understand format that also compares the activity to a previous time period. Two of the key measures you will want to review are page views and unique page views. According to the Google website:

> A pageview is defined as a view of a page on your site that is being tracked by the Analytics tracking code. If a visitor hits reload after reaching the page, this will be counted as an additional pageview. If a user navigates to a different page and then returns to the original page, a second pageview will be recorded as well.
>
> A unique pageview aggregates pageviews that are generated by the same user during the same session. A unique pageview represents the number of sessions during which that page was viewed one or more times.

This means that you are likely to have many more pageviews than unique pageviews, but both of the measurements help you understand what people like about your blog. They show if the content you post is relevant to visitors, and it also shows what types of content attracts new visitors. Delia Mendenhall measures every post she makes on her blog with Google

Analytics, and refers to previous popular posts in other posts to keep her audience interested and involved.

Other information available via Google Analytics includes:

- Follower measures
    - *Unique visitors*: You can measure how many people at your site are new and how many are returning. You want to be constantly growing your visits while making sure people are returning to see what is new at your site. If you are not regularly increasing your visitors, think about why. Are you directing people to your website in all your social media? Is your website included on your profiles on social media? Have you optimized your page for search (see Chapter 6)? Jennifer Osborn (2010) provides these benchmarks for business blogs:

        - Average traffic benchmarks for a Small Business Blog = 1,000 to 2,000 visitors per month
        - For Mid-Sized Business = 10,000 to 20,000 visitors per month
        - For Large, Enterprise-Sized Clients = 50,000 to 100,000 blog visitors per month.

    - *Page views*: This is a measurement of how "deep" people are going in to your site. If you have multiple pages, you want people to visit more than just the first or home page. If you have a website with multiple pages, and people aren't visiting one or two pages, take a look at those pages and try to figure out what the problem might be. Della Mendenhall (Gillespie Florist) noticed that one of her pages was titled "Corporate Gifts" and received almost no hits. She looked at the page, and realized that the content on that page was primarily gift baskets, which could be a corporate gift but could just as easily be a personal gift. She changed the page name to "Gift Baskets" and saw a huge increase in the number of visits to that page.

    - *How people found your blog*: Google shows you where readers were prior to visiting your page. You may also get this information via a poll on your site; many blog programs allow you to quickly and easily post simple polls. One poll might ask people how they found your site, giving them choices such as:

- Through your Facebook page
- Through your Twitter feed
- Through your website
- Through a Google search
- Other (please indicate)

- Engagement measures
  - *Time spent on site*: You can also see how long, in total, people spend on your site. In general, people spend less than a minute on any given page of a site, so if you see that the average time spent on any page is 45 or 50 seconds, you should not get discouraged! If people are not spending a lot of time on your site, think about why. Do you need to update the content more, or perhaps put up more interesting content like a video or some photographs? Try different types of content and monitor which ones encourage people to spend more time on the site. Your goal should be for people to spend 2–5 minutes per visit on your blog.
  - *Number of comments*: For your blog as on Facebook, you want to see if people are participating by leaving comments at your blog, and you'll want to see how comments change over time. Track which types of posts are generating the most comments, and try to increase your use of those types of posts. One great idea is to ask questions and get your followers to respond.
  - *Quality of comments*: Google Analytics does not measure this, but you want to monitor the types of comments people are leaving at your blog. Are they stimulating discussion and encouraging others to get involved in the site? This is what you want to achieve. Getting involved in the comments by thanking people or asking them to go into more detail can also improve the quality of comments.
  - *Downloads*: If you offer something downloadable on your site, check how often and for what types of offerings downloads occur.
- Mention measures
  - TweetMeme: install the TweetMeme (http://www.tweetmeme .com) program on your blog and visitors can tweet about your

post to their Twitter network. Track which posts are most popular given the number of tweets.

- Conversation measures
  - ○ If you mention a specific product or service in a blog post, track how often that produce or service is purchased both before the post and after. Justin Stobb (All American Auto) discusses a range of different auto repairs on his blog posts, and compares the requested services to the services discussed in his blog to track any upticks.
- Other types of measures
  - ○ *Measures at review sites*: Plan to regularly monitor user opinion sites like Yelp (review Chapter 2 for more information) to track how number and sentiment of reviews change over time.
  - ○ *Social media mentions*: Keep track of conversations not directly related to your social media sites via social mention and track how the number and sentiments of reviews change over time.

A Word of Caution

These tools are just that: tools. Quantitative measurements are functional tools, but they won't supplant your being involved in the actual conversations. Jesse Yu (Qoola) sees that these trending tools are limited, especially if it is the only way that you are getting data about conversations. He sees that monitoring word of mouth and in-person conversations and connections are more important to build his business. Adam Cuppy (Dutch Bros.) agrees, and stated that "the number one tool we use are personal impressions . . . did customers say something that indicates they saw the social media?" Justin Stobb (All American Auto) instructs all of his employees to ask new customers how they found out about his repair shop, and uses that information to direct his own efforts.

Key Chapter Insights

- Use measurement data to check the effectiveness of your social media campaign and do it regularly. Use benchmarks to measure success— e.g., how your followers grow (or decline) each month, and compare this data to competitors' followers as well.

- Measuring social media can include ROI/monetization but should focus on the amount of social activity generated. Social media is more of a brand involvement medium than a response medium.

- Understand and use tools available from social media applications like Facebook and Twitter, but use your own evaluations to bring a greater level of understanding to the measurements. For example, the number of re-tweets itself gives some degree of understanding, but re-tweets can also be a valuable guide to topics that generate the most interest via Twitter.

- The application Qwitter allows you to determine when you have lost a follower, and what tweet that they read last. This can be helpful in learning what topics might be turning off followers.

- Measurement tools are essential for evaluating social media success, but nothing replaces spending time on your sites to see and feel the reaction you are getting to your information.

Getting Started

- If you're brand new to social media: Set up an account on Google Analytics and add the code to your website and blog. The Google Analytics website has step-by-step instructions on how to do this.

- If you are familiar with social media: Start to track the number of followers at each of your social media sites, and track the change in followers every week. Compare this change with the types of messages you've posted to help you determine which ones are generating the highest increase in followers.

- If you are ready to move to the next level: Look specifically at comments and track whether the quality of the comments is improving. If not, start responding more often to comments to get more information or to get the follower to talk more.

- Nothing takes the place of asking customers how they found you.

8

Social Media Audits: A Tool to Create Your Strategy

We have covered a lot of the social media landscape in this book: how to listen to what people are saying, how to set goals and measure results, how to establish and build a community in the social sphere, and what types of messages to consider using. We have mainly focused on your business in these discussions, and we hope by now you have many ideas that you want to try.

In addition, throughout the book, we have recommended that you check out what your competitors are doing in the social sphere as well. This is important for several reasons.

- You can see where your competitors are putting their efforts in social media. This means your competitors think their customers are there, and so maybe you should think about being there as well.

- You can use what people are talking about in your competitors' social media space to check out your own business. Are there complaints about a competitor that people might have about your business as well? Is there something you can do about that complaint? What do people say positively about your competitors? Can they say that about your business, too, or do you have to do something to improve in that area?

- You can see the types of conversations that engage customers at your competitors' sites. These conversations can spark ideas about conversations at your own site.

- You can use this information to set goals for your own social media campaign.

- You can use this information as benchmarks to measure your future success.

You are probably already doing some of this informally: you may be checking out your competition's Facebook pages every so often, and you may also see what customers are saying about your competitors on rating sites such as Yelp and Insider Pages. Doing this type of informal monitoring on a regular basis may give you all you need to have a great social media strategy.

Some business owners may prefer to undertake a more formal review by conducting a social media audit. A social media audit is the process used to identify brand-building and business-development activities (Wainright 2010). An audit surveys the social media landscape to find out what customers, influencers, partners, and employees are participating in on the social web. Like other types of audits, social media audits are key for identifying priorities, benchmarking previous efforts, and planning for future efforts; the same applies to social media.

In this chapter, we provide you with a series of instructions on how to audit different areas of the social media space. Undertaking all of the audits at one time may seem daunting, so we recommend that you start with an audit for an area that you do not know much about. If you are unfamiliar with ratings sites, for example, try the "Social Listening" audit. If you have not spent time thinking about search engine optimization, start with that audit. The bottom line is that after you conduct a social media audit, you will be able to make better business decisions when it comes to social media. You will be able to gather enough data from your own campaigns to help you improve your online marketing (Owyang 2009).

Starting a Social Media Audit

Regardless of which type of audit you chose to perform, you should make a few decisions upfront that will apply to any type of audit that you do.

Develop a List of Competitors

The key to a good social media audit is identifying two or three competitors. One competitor (Competitor A) should be similar in size and scope to your business, based on metrics such as:

- Size of business in terms of sales
- Square feet of retail space

- Range of products
- Number of locations

The second (Competitor B) should be a larger competitor: it could be a national or global giant that you do not consider a direct competitor but a market force nonetheless. The third competitor (Competitor C) could either be a business operating on a smaller scale or another competitor similar in size and scope to your business (Wainright 2010).

Pick a Time Period

The audit will cover a specified period of time for your business and your competitors. How long a time period should you select? As a starting point, use the most recent full month. If you are starting the auditing process on August 5, then, you would use the previous month of July for your audit. For optimal insights, you will want to be able to examine at least 10 posts in at least one social network site for each your competitors. For example, if Competitor A uses Facebook and posted 18 comments in July, then you are all set to use July as your time period. If Competitor A posted only six times, though, you may have to use both June and July to have at least 10 comments.

Once you figure out a time period using one social media site, use that for your investigations of the other social media sites, even if there are fewer than 10 posts on the other social media sites.

Put Aside Half an Hour to Spend Online

Each of our audits is designed to be completed in one sitting, and we anticipate each audit will take about 30 minutes or less to conduct. It will work best if you can dedicate a block of 30 minutes to do the audit instead of trying to keep revisiting it in 5- or 10-minute blocks.

The Online Listening Audit

Keeping tabs on conversations at review sites give you a quick snapshot of customer praises and concerns (see Table 8.1).

- Select one review site, like Yelp.com or Insider Pages.com (see Chapter 2 for a list of other sites you could use), and examine your reviews on that site.

TABLE 8.1[1]
Social Media Audit
Online Listening

Review Site:	Your Business	Competitor A	Competitor B	Competitor C
Time Period:				
# Reviews in Time Period				
Mix of Positive/Negative Reviews				
Types of Positive Comments				
Types of Negative Comments				
Business Responses				

- Count the number of reviews during the designated time period, add that to the chart, and indicate the total number of posts as well.
- Examine the posts during the designated time period and assess the mix of positive and negative, making notes on trends in the comments for both positive and negative on the chart.
- Repeat this process for each of your three competitors.

This information will quickly give you an idea of the different places people are talking about your business and businesses like yours, as well as give you an idea of what good things and bad things people are saying. Ask yourself these questions:

- *Do I have a positive presence on review sites?* If you have more negative reviews than positive reviews, look at the specific problems mentioned and see how you can change your business to address the negative reviews. Then promote these changes throughout your social media.
- *Do I agree with what people are saying about my business on review sites?* If you find that you do not agree with more than one or two

---

[1]We include additional copies of these tables in the Appendix for you to photocopy and use. For electronic copies, visit our website (http://www.grabbinggreen.com).

TABLE 8.2
Social Media Audit
Social Media Overview

Business Name: Time Period:							
	# Fol-lowers (a)	Total Posts by Business (b)	Post Subjects (c)	Total Posts by Followers (d)	Post Subjects (e)	Total Com-ments (f)	Post Subjects That Gener-ated Com-ments (g)
Website		x	x	x	x	x	
Blog				x	x		
Facebook							
Twitter				x	x		
YouTube	x			x	x		
Flickr	x			x	x		
Other							

posts, consider setting up a business account and replying to the negative posters to correct the misinformation.

- *Do people talk about the things I want them to talk about? If not, what would I prefer that they talk about?* Think about what you would like them to talk about in terms of product quality, convenience, range of products, service quality, and the like, and include those stories and ideas in your social media messages.

- *Do the review sites suggest that my competitors have the same strengths that I have?* If so, be sure you are talking about these strengths more often than your competitors are.

- *Are the negative aspects of my competitor's business a strength in my business?* If so, consider talking about these strengths regularly in your social media messages.

The Social Networking Site Overview Audit

The purpose of this audit is to give you a quick snapshot of the total social media presence of your business and your competitors (Table 8.2). You will want to make several copies of this chart: one for your business, and one for each of the competitors you are auditing.

- The first chart you will complete is for your business. Enter the name of your business and the time period you will use for your audit.

- Visit your website and access whatever analytics you can (see Chapter 7 for a discussion of analytics).

- In the top row, enter whatever analytics you can access. Look primarily at the number of followers (or perhaps registered users or visitors) in box a. We have placed an "x" in other boxes in the row because they aren't relevant.

- If you have a blog, visit that next. Again, your analytics can show you how many followers or visitors you have (place in box a).
    - Count up the total number of blog posts you have made during the specific time period, and indicate the types of subjects your posts discussed (boxes c and d). Subjects can include "new products," "promotions," "employee news," "store news," and the like.
    - Skip the next two boxes and indicate the total number of comments during your posts that were entered during the time period in box g, and the subjects that generated the most comments in box h.

- Visit your Facebook site. If you don't have a Facebook site yet, we bet you are ready to start one. Visit Chapter 4a for instructions on how to do so.
    - Indicate your followers in box a, your total wall posts in box b, and the subjects in box c.
    - If other people post on your wall, enter the total number of posts by others in box d and the subjects in box e.
    - Count up the comments in box f and the types of posts that generate comments in box g. These can be the subjects that generate the most comments, regardless of whether you started the discussion or others started the discussion.

- Move to Twitter, and repeat the process.
    - Total followers go in box a, total posts in box b, and types of subjects in box c.

- o Skip to box f, and instead of comments, count the number of posts you made that have been re-tweeted. To do this, click the "Retweets" link on the right-hand side of your Twitter page.
- o Indicate the subjects of the posts that generated comments in box h.
- If you are using YouTube and/or Flickr, go to those pages and see how many videos and/or images you posted during the time period.
  - o Enter the appropriate number in box b for each service.
  - o Check to see if people commented on any of your videos and/or images. If so, count the total number (enter in box g) and then indicate the subject of the videos or images that generated comments in box h.
- If there is another service you use, enter relevant information in the last row.
- Repeat this process for each of your competitors.

Looking over this information, see if the data indicates what your "nerve center" is. Is it what you think it is? If so, that is a good thing. If not, spend a bit of time figuring out why there might be some disconnects. Are you splitting your energy into multiple sites and not focusing in one place? If so, take time to figure out a nerve center: the social networking site where you will place most of your time and energy. Revisit Chapter 3 and figure it out.

Then ask yourself these questions:

1. *Are my competitors strong where I am strong?* Are there sites where we have very similar efforts in terms of posting and other types of content? If the answer is no, then you have a competitive advantage in that social media space, and you should utilize it as much as possible. If the answer is yes, you need to make sure you keep a strong competitive presence relative to your competitors; monitor often to make sure.

2. *Are my competitors strong where I am weak?* If the answer is yes, then you need to make a decision: will you continue in that area, or will you put your energy in a different area?

3. *Are my competitors weak where I am weak?* If you answerd yes, you can either strengthen your presence there or recognize that the media will always be a secondary medium for you and your competitors (you will want to re-audit this every so often in order to see if this stays true). If you answered no, then you might want to consider strengthening your presence.

The Search Engine Optimization Audit

Are you using the best words and phrases on your website and in all your social media network sites? This audit (Table 8.3) will help you determine how well you do that relative to your competition. (See Chapter 5 for a more compete discussion.)

• Begin by thinking of keywords or phrases you think best direct people to your social media site (or what keywords you plan to use). Enter those keywords and phrases in every box underneath box a, in Table 8.3.

• Examine each social media site that you use to count up the number of times you used those keywords.

• Examine the social media sites of your three competitors to see if (and how often) they use those keywords and phrases.

• Ask yourself whether you use the words more or less often than your competitors.

  ○ If you use them on a par with competitors, or if you are using them more often, you are probably doing well with site optimization.

  ○ If you are using them less often, you might need to work on your site optimization a bit. Chapter 5 can help guide you through that process.

The Nerve Center Audit

Your nerve center (Chapter 3) is where you are (or will be) spending most of your time and energy in the social sphere. It is very important to know what your competitors are doing in the same social space as your nerve center.

TABLE 8.3
Social Media Audit
Search Engine Optimization

Your Business:				
Key Words/Phrases (a)	# Times Used in Time Period			
	Web	Facebook	Twitter	Blog

Competitor A				
Key Words/Phrases	# Times Used in Time Period			
	Web	Facebook	Twitter	Blog

Competitor B				
Key Words/Phrases	# Times Used in Time Period			
	Web	Facebook	Twitter	Blog

Competitor C				
Key Words/Phrases	# Times Used in Time Period			
	Web	Facebook	Twitter	Blog

TABLE 8.4
Social Media Audit
Nerve Center Audit: Facebook

Feature	Your Business	Competitor A	Competitor B	Competitor C
Who authors? Number of voices?				
Profile/info page quality?				
Outgoing links? Where?				
Average updates per week				
Use of media other than text				
Other				

The Facebook Nerve Center Audit

This audit can help you examine both your own Facebook presence or nerve center and that of your competitors. It may also help to review our discussion of Facebook metrics in Chapter 7. Be sure to enter the time period and competitors in Table 8.4.

- During your selected time period, count the different number of people who are posting on the wall. Enter the number.

- If people other than yourself are posting on your wall (or to say another way, if the number you entered is greater than 1), enter the types of people who are posting (how many employees, how many customers).

- Look at the Info page on Facebook sites and examine the quality of your profile and that of your competitors. Indicate the range of information included on your profile: write down what specific information you and your competitors include.

> 8.1 Action Idea: Remember that the "average" business posts on Facebook six times each week. Even if you are posting at the same frequency as your competitors, if you are all posting two or three times per week, there is room to increase your posting frequency, which can lead to more followers and more engagement.

- Look at the use of links.

  o Enter how many outgoing links are used on your and your competitors' pages during the time period.

  o Enter a summary of where people are directed to with their links. Are links going to the business website, other types of websites, and the like?

- Calculate the average number of posts per week (total posts divided by total weeks in your audit).

- Look at whether the sites use media other than text—videos, images, etc.—and indicate the number and subjects of different media.

- If you notice other interesting uses of Facebook, indicate that in the "other" line.

Once this is complete, compare your activity to that of your competitors. You can use this information to develop your social media goals for Facebook. Some questions to consider are:

- *Do you have a number of different people posting, especially if your competitors do?* If not, you should set a goal of encouraging others to post in addition to you or whoever your primary poster is.

- *Is your profile as complete as your competitors?* If not, take a few moments to bring your profile up to the level of detail as your competitors.

- *Do you post at least as often, if not more often, than your competitors?* If not, then you will need to set a goal of increasing your posts.

- *What is your share of voice overall?* Total the number of posts made during the time period for you and your competitors. Then take the number of posts you have made divided by total posts to estimate your share of voice. Set a plan to build your share of voice to about 40 percent among your competitors.[2]

_____

[2.]Here is an example: You make 10 posts on your Facebook page in a 30-day period, Competitor A makes 15, Competitor B makes 5, and Competitor C makes 7. Your share of voice is 10/37, or 27 percent, and Competitor A's is about 40 percent. If you increase your number of posts to 15 over 30 days, and everyone else stays the same, your share of voice will increase to 15/42, or 36 percent, and Competitor A will be the same.

- *Are you posting links, videos, and images at the same pace as your competitors?* If not, your goal should be to increase posting in that area. The share-of-voice formula can be used for this as well.

- *Are you posting things in the same subject areas as your competitors?* If not, consider why they are posting in these subject areas and consider whether they are beneficial areas for you as well. You can also estimate your share of voice on specific topics: repeat the share-of-voice measurement above analyzing the frequency of a specific topic, such as new products, customer service, etc. Again, your plan should be to build your share of voice to about 40 percent among your competitors.

TABLE 8.5
Social Media Audit
Nerve Center Audit: Twitter

Feature	Your Business	Competitor A	Competitor B	Competitor C
Biography/background?				
Frequency of tweets?				
Outgoing links: Frequency and to where?				
Conversations/engagement?				
Other?				

The Twitter Nerve Center Audit

This audit can help you examine both your own Twitter presence or nerve center and that of your competitors. It may also help to review our discussion of Twitter metrics in Chapter 7. Be sure to enter the time period and competitors in Table 8.5.

- Take a look at Twitter profiles, and indicate the types of information included in the profile for you and your competitors on the first row.

- Calculate the average number of times you and your competitors post a tweet each week; enter that on the second row.

- Count the number of tweets that contained a link to some place outside of Twitter.

o   Assess what types of places both you and your competitors link to: it is likely that many tweets will link to either the business Facebook site or web page.

> 8.2 Action Idea: Do you recall that the "average" business tweets on Twitter six times per day? Even if you are leading the competitive pack with four tweets per day, there is still room for an additional tweet or two to have a strong voice in the Twittersphere.

- Assess the types of conversations that are happening between the business and other customers. You may have to look at some Twitter pages of people whom you are not following, especially if the tweet from a competitor starts with the "@" symbol, which means it is going directly to an individual.

- Get an idea as to whether competitors are using tweets for thank-yous, to answer questions about products or services, or to solve customer problems and address customer complaints.

In order to set some social media goals for your Twitter nerve center, you can consider these questions:

- Is my profile as information rich as possible, and as information rich as those of my competitors? If not, take a few moments to craft a stronger social media profile.

- Am I tweeting at least as often, if not more, than my competitors? You can calculate your share of voice for Twitter by totaling the number of posts made during the time period for you and your competitors. Then take the number of posts you have made divided by total posts to estimate your share of voice. Set a plan to build your share of voice to about 40 percent among your competitors.[3]

- Do I link to my Facebook page and website? If not, what types of messages can I include that direct people to these sites?

[3.] Here is an example: You tweet 20 different times during a 30-day period, Competitor A makes 18, Competitor B makes 42, and Competitor C makes 4. Your share of voice is 20/84 or 24 percent, and Competitor B's is about 50 percent. If you increase your number of tweets to 38 over 30 days, and everyone else stays the same, your share of voice will increase to 38/102 or 37 percent, and Competitor B will be 41 percent.

- Do I link to pages my customers will find interesting? If not, what types of information can I include in searches for information about your business (such as through Google Alerts) to find links to share with my followers?
- Do I have conversations at the same frequency as my competitors? Do I engage customers as well as my competitors? When reading over my competitors' tweets, would I recommend they do something differently? Do I need to do that, too? Sometimes it is easier to see our faults reflected in others' activities, and we can take that information and learn from it.

TABLE 8.6
Social Media Audit
Nerve Center Audit: Blogs

Feature	Your Business	Competitor A	Competitor B	Competitor C
Quality and topics of posts?				
Number and responses to comments?				
Outgoing links?				
Types of media used				

The Blog Nerve Center Audit

This audit can help you examine both your own blog presence or nerve center and that of your competitors. It may also help to review our discussion of blog metrics in Chapter 7. Be sure to enter the time period and competitors in Table 8.6.

- Look at the different types of subjects of posts and indicate the range of topics on the form
  - Assess the quality of posts: whether they are well written, are interesting to read, and how well they relate to customers and connect customers to the business.
- Examine comments to the blogs. Estimate an average number of comments to blogs, and then evaluate how engaged the commenters seem

to be with the post. Are they writing lengthy comments or just posting one or two words?

o   Assess outgoing links. To what types of places are they directing people?

o   Assess what media other than text are used on blogs (images, videos, and the like), and look at what types of topics they cover.

Ask yourself the following questions about your findings:

> **8.3 Action Idea: How often should you post?** Remember the average business posts two or three times a week on their blog. You should be posting at least that often, and more frequently if your competitors are posting more frequently. Remember, a good blog post can be six or seven sentences; it does not have to be *War and Peace!*

- *Do I discuss a range of subjects?* If you are primarily talking about a single topic, such as promotions and special offers, you should consider setting a goal of adding variety to your subjects in order to appeal to more people.

- *Do I talk about subjects similar to my competitors?* If your competitors are talking about a range of different subjects, and some of these subjects might appeal to your customers, then consider adding some of these subjects to your blog. You can perform the share of voice analysis on different types of subjects.[4]

- *Are posts well written?* Try to look objectively at the different posts at different blogs. React to which ones engage you as a reader, and try to identify the elements that caused you to connect to the blog post. Was it the vividness of the language, the sense of the individual writing the post, or the depth of information? Try to integrate such characteristics into your blog posts.

[4.]Here's an example: You make 8 posts on your blog during a 30-day period about new products, Competitor A makes 2, Competitor B makes 2, and Competitor C makes 1. Your share of voice is 8/13, or 62 percent. You make 1 post on your blog during a 30-day period about industry news, and your competitors each make 3. You share of voice on industry news is 10 percent. In this situation, consider increasing the number of industry posts and decreasing (or combining) new product posts.

- *What types of posts get people to comment?* Beyond that, what types of posts get people to write longer, more interesting and engaging comments, as opposed to a brief comment like "Thanks for that information"? This information can be valuable to use when deciding what types of subjects to post about.

- *What types of media, other than text, tend to be used?* If your competitors are using images and videos, think about integrating these things into your blog posts as well.

TABLE 8.7
Social Media Audit
Action Plan

Action Plan	Notes	Priority
Create SNS presence		
Improve SNS presence		
Improve engagement		
Improve number/quality of voices		
Increase followers		
Improve responses to postings at rating sites		

Setting Your Social Media Agenda

By understanding the social media sphere using different types of audits, you have probably generated a list of goals for your social media activities. The final step for the audit is to organize these goals and to develop priorities and action steps to achieve the goals. You can organize that information in Table 8.7. Enter the goals you developed at each stage of the audit in the appropriate categories in Table 8.7. For example, if your goal is to increase the number of posts on your Facebook wall, write that goal under "Improve SNS presence." If your goal is to start a Twitter program, write that goal under "Create SNS presence." If your goal is to post a variety of topics to get more people involved at a social network site, write that down under "improve engagement."

Now that your goals are organized, you can set priorities for what you want to achieve. What we would recommend is to focus first on whichever social media site you have designed as your nerve center, and make sure you have a strong presence at your nerve center. As a second priority, we would recommend that you have a good handle on the conversations happening at ratings sites like Insider Pages and Yelp. Not only are these important conversations to hear, but these ratings sites often turn up high in the results in Google searches. Addressing any problematic comments proactively will show your business in its best light when people go searching for businesses in your category. Of course, your priorities will be affected by your competition and by the amount of time you can devote to your social media activities.

Key Chapter Insights

o   Doing a social media audit will help you make better use of your social media time and efforts.

o   When doing the audit, check the activities of various sizes of competitors.

o   Conduct the audit during a recent period (for example, over the last few weeks) when enough activity has occurred to measure results.

o   The audit should provide an idea of the scope and number of places in which people are talking about businesses such as yours. It will also provide a sense of positive and negative things being said in your business category, things that you can watch out for.

o   The audit should help you determine where the nerve center or focus of social media activity is for your type of business. Continuing audits will allow you to compare your nerve center with those of your competitors.

o   Analyzing keyword usage in your social media presence will show you if you are effectively optimizing your social media presence.

o   Conducting regular audits every six months will give you the key steps to enhance your social media program.

Some Final Thoughts

Once you set your goals, remember to continue to monitor your social media presence to see how you are performing. At least once per month, check to see how you are doing in terms of

8.4 Action Idea: We recommend you select three important areas in your social media presence and repeat the social media audit every quarter.

building your social presence and energizing your community. In particular, it is important to re-audit those areas in which you were underperforming relative to your competition to assess how you are performing.

As we have now reached the end of the book, we do not have any other specific next steps for you except to go for it! Every individual we spoke with for this book made a similar statement—that now is the time to try social media and see how it can affect your business. Here is their advice:

- "I would say the first thing is just to jump in. I think it is OK to just jump in and make some mistakes. There's no right or wrong way to do it. Just being in the game is the first thing" (Brian Mason, SKP-Popcorn).

- "Pay attention to how other people are using social media; you'll learn by osmosis and be able to figure it out on your own" (Kelli Matthews, Café Yumm!).

- "It's easy. My whole theory in marketing is even if I get one customer, that's a customer I can have for life" (Lisa Hartwick, Hartwick's Kitchen Store).

- "Get involved. There's piles and piles of information about people and customers and their product that's being discussed every day, and you can benefit from that" (Mark Beauchamp, Café Yumm!).

- "It is up to you to get as engaged as you want to be" (Jesse Yu, Qoola).

- "So much of it is a personal comfort zone, and obviously you're only going to be successful in a medium if you're comfortable with it as a person" (Erica Leaf, Imagine Graphics)

What do we recommend? It is simple: Get started today. Pick a social media that appeals to you and spend 10 or 15 minutes checking it out and seeing what it is like. You may find it confusing or unwieldy, and that is not a problem. Tomorrow, pick another social media site and spend a few minutes there. We guarantee that eventually you will find a social media space that feels like home for you and your business, and you can start to build your online word of mouth from there.

Finally, we wish you all good luck with your efforts!

Appendix

Appendix A

Social Media Audit
Online Listening

Review Site:	Your Business	Competitor A	Competitor B	Competitor C
Time Period:				
# Reviews in Time Period				
Total # Reviews				
Mix of Positive/Negative Reviews				
Types of Positive Comments				
Types of Negative Comments				
Business Responses				

Appendix B

Social Media Audit
Social Media Overview

Business Name: Time Period:							
	# Fol- lowers (a)	Total Posts by Business (b)	Post Subjects (c)	Total Posts by Followers (d)	Post Subjects (e)	Total Com- ments (f)	Post Sub- jects That Generated Comments (g)
Website		x	x	x	x	x	
Blog				x	x		
Facebook							
Twitter				x	x		
YouTube	x			x	x		
Flickr	x			x	x		
Other							

Appendix C

Social Media Audit
Search Engine Optimization

Your Business:				
Key Words/Phrases (a)	Times used in Time Period			
	Web	Facebook	Twitter	Blog

Competitor A				
Key Words/Phrases	# Times Used in Time Period			
	Web	Facebook	Twitter	Blog

Competitor B				
Key Words/Phrases	# Times Used in Time Period			
	Web	Facebook	Twitter	Blog

Competitor C				
Key Words/Phrases	# Times Used in Time Period			
	Web	Facebook	Twitter	Blog

Appendix D

Social Media Audit
Nerve Center Audit: Facebook

Facebook				
Feature	Your Business	Competitor A	Competitor B	Competitor C
Who authors? Number of voices?				
Profile/info page quality?				
Outgoing links? Where?				
Average updates per week				
Use of media other than text				
Other				

Appendix E

Social Media Audit
Nerve Center Audit: Twitter

Twitter				
Feature	Your Business	Competitor A	Competitor B	Competitor C
Biography/background?				
Frequency of tweets?				
Outgoing links: Frequency and to where?				
Conversations/engagement?				
Other?				

Appendix F

Social Media Audit
Nerve Center Audit: Blogs

Blogs				
Feature	*Your Business*	*Competitor A*	*Competitor B*	*Competitor C*
Quality and topics of posts?				
Number and responses to comments?				
Outgoing links?				
Types of media used				

Appendix G

Social Media Audit
Action Plan

Action Plan	*Notes*	*Priority*
Create SNS presence		
Improve SNS presence		
Improve engagement		
Improve number/quality of voices		
Increase followers		
Improve responses to postings at rating sites		

References

Albright, Mary Ann. 2010. "Foursquare Keeps Friends on the Same Path." *The Columbian*, http://www.columbian.com/news/2010/jun/27/foursquare-keeps-friends-on-same-path/.

Ambler, George. 2006. "Setting SMART Objectives." *The Practice of Leadership*, http://www.thepracticeofleadership.net/2006/03/11/setting-smart-objectives/.

Authority Domains. 2010. "Five Free Simple Social Media Benchmarks." *Authority Domains*, http://www.authoritydomains.com/blogs/social-media-marketing/5-free-simple-social-media-benchmarks.php.

Brogan, Chris. 2009. "Are You a Trust Agent." *Chris Brogan Blog*, http://www.chrisbrogan.com/are-you-a-trust-agent/.

Brogan, Chris. 2009. "Best Fits for Social Media." *Chris Brogan Blog*, http://www.chrisbrogan.com/best-fits-for-social-media-in-the-sales-cycle/

Campbell, Debbie. 2010. "What's the Value in Your Website's Sitemap to Search Engines?" *Marketing for Success*, http://www.marketingforsuccess.com/blog/web-marketing/search-engines/sitemap-search-engines/.

Citibank. 2010. "Citibank Survey Finds Small Businesses Not Leveraging Online Tools to Drive Their Business." *Business Wire*, http://www.businesswire.com/portal/site/home/permalink/?ndmViewId=news_view&newsId=20100421005319&newsLang=en.

comScore. 2009. "GroupM Search and comScore Release Study on the Interplay Between Search Marketing and Social Media." *comScore*, http://www.comscore.com/Press_Events/Press_Releases/2009/10/GroupM

_Search_and_comScore_Release_Study_on_the_Interplay_Between _Search_Marketing_and_Social_Media.

Emarketer.com. 2010. "Double Digit Growth for Local Mobile Audience." *Emarketer*, http://www.emarketer.com.

Kaplan Andreas M., and Michael Haenlein. 2010. "Users of the World, Unite! The Challenges and Opportunities of Social Media." *Business Horizons*, 53, no. 1: 59–68.

M+R Strategic Services. 2010. *2010 Benchmarks Study*. http://www .e-benchmarksstudy.com/2010.html.

Maxwell, Norma. 2010. "A Simple Guide to Choosing the Right Keywords for Your Business." *Biznik*, http://biznik.com/articles.

Osbore, Jennifer. 2010. "Business Blogs Benchmarks," *Search Engine People*, http://www.searchenginepeople.com/blog/business-blog-benchmarks.html.

Owyang, Jeremiah. 2009. "The Importance of Social Media Audits." *Web Strategist*, available: http://www.web-strategist.com/blog/2009/07/28/ the-importance-of-a-social-media-audits/.

Pick, Tom. 2010. "Eight Common Mistakes in B2B Social Marketing." *HubSpot*, http://blog.hubspot.com/blog/tabid/6307/bid/5668/8 -Common-Mistakes-in-B2B-Social-Media-Marketing.aspx.

Rosenthal, Morris. 2010. *Content SEO for Writers: Creating Original Websites That Work for Search Engines Because They Work for People*, New York: Foner Books.

Sernovitz, Andy. 2006. *Word of Mouth Marketing: How Smart Companies Get People Talking*. New York: Kaplan Business.

Vermeiren, Jan. 2010. "Six More Tips for your LinkedIn Profile." *Marketing for Success*, http://www.marketingforsuccess.com/blog/web-marketing/ social-media/linkedin-profile-2/.

Wainright, Jeannie. 2010. "Elements of a Social Media Audit." *Suite 101*, http://marketingpr.suite101.com/article.cfm/elements-of-a-social-media -audit#ixzz0uRnsT300.

Index

('n' indicates a note; 't' indicates a table)

Achievable, SMART goal
   methodology, 6
Action Idea
   competition monitoring, 16
   complementary businesses, 118
   daily conversation monitoring, 23
   daily Twitter postings, 161
   experience to write about, 24
   fun video, 80
   goals and measures, 136
   Google Alerts, 47
   industry news, 117
   LinkedIn profile, 123
   lo-so networks, 111
   negative review responses, 29
   quarterly social media
     audit, 165
   reading posts out loud, 78
   re-tweeting goal, 141
   search words, 102
   searches Google Alerts and
     Social Mention, 140
   site integration, 49
   social glue determination, 73
   special offers, 85
   staying on tract, 84
   stories, 75
   surveys, 60
   unique feature, 105
   weekly blog postings, 163
   weekly Facebook postings, 158
Action monitoring, 15
Action plan, 171
Activity, Facebook measure, 137
Advertisement purchasing, 52, 63
All Wheel Drive Auto, Seattle, 9,
   10, 74, 99
Angie's List, 20
Authority, search rating, 100

BackType, 22
Bad conversations, 24–29
Banner advertisements, 3
Beauchamp, Marc, 7, 13, 53,
   60–61, 166
Benchmarks, 135
Betts, Mitch, 133
"Bidding" system, 52
Bing, search, 97, 99
Bing Local Listing Center, 110

Bisinger, Jillian, photographer, 7,
    47, 54, 58–59, 80, 98,
    103, 104
Bit.ly, Twitter tracking tool, 142
Biznik, 121
"Black hat SEO," 103–104
Blackberry, check-ins, 110
Bleeding Heart Bakery, The,
    Chicago, 10, 29
Blog
    nerve center audit, 162t,
        162–164, 171
    social media overview audit,
        153t, 154
Blogger (provider), 3
    website building, 98
Bloggers, 15, 16, 36
Blogging, 3, 33, 47–49
    metrics, 143–146
    site creation, 35–38
    success tips , 39
    and website updating, 104
"Blogging Nurseryman," 47, 117
Blue Moon Burgers in Seattle,
    10, 77
Bluedot, 22
BNI (Business Network
    International), 115, 121
Boardreader, 22–23
BoardTracker, 22
Bohan, Dan, 7, 102, 103
Boneham, Rupert, 54
Brand-building, 150
Brands, in daily conversations,
    13, 14
Bright Kite, 4
Brogan, Chris, 5, 15

*Building Buzz to Beat the Big
    Boys,* (O'Leary and
    Sheehan), 55, 72
Bulletin board monitoring, 22
Burke's Bar, Yonkers, New York,
    10, 77
Business mission, and social
    engagement, 72
Business networks, 120–122
    benefits, 116–120
    contacts, 123–124
    discussion seeding, 125
    local promotion, 125
    maintenance, 126
    profile creation, 122–123
    questions and answers,
        124–125
Business page, Facebook, 64,
    66–67
Business-development
    activities, 150
Business-to-business (B2B), 115

Café Yumm!, 7, 13, 25, 51, 53,
    55, 73
CD World, 8, 46, 49, 88
"Chatter" feature, 22. *See also*
    YackTrack
Citibank, social networking use
    study, 2
Clickthroughs, 52
Clutter, Twitter, 46, 47
Colla, Beth, 7, 54, 82
Comments, Google
    Analytics, 144
Communication, in social media,
    71–72

Community
  building, 50–52, 75–76
  managing, 59–60
  staff involvement, 60–61
Company news, website
    update, 109
Competition
  as benchmark, 135
  monitoring, 16, 43, 149–150
  negative posts by, 27
  Yelp, 19
Competitors, presence
    auditing, 156
Complementary businesses, 118
comScore, 98
Controversial/noncontroversial
    topics, 56, 83
Conversations
  bad, 24–29
  cocktail party, 78–79
  daily checking, 21
  Facebook measures, 139
  good, 23–24
  listing to, 15
  measures, 135, 146
  Twitter measures, 141–142
Corporate blogs, 34
CraigsList, 86
Criticism, and improvement,
    13, 14
Cross promotion development,
    118–119
Cuppy, Adam, 7, 24, 26, 45, 50,
    52, 55, 78, 80, 83, 84, 87, 89,
    98, 111, 146
Customer created commercials, 84
Customer segments, 77

Customers
  creative, 84
  pictures, 89
  responding to, 25, 56
  user-review sites, 18

Daily active users, Facebook
    measure, 137
Data availability, 134
Deck, Somer, 7, 52, 54, 81,
    141, 142
Deleting content, 59
Demographics, Facebook
    measure, 137
deviantArt, 4
Digital messages, 3
Dislikes, Facebook measure, 137
Dutch Bros., 7, 24, 26, 45, 50, 52,
    55, 73
Dynamic media presence, 41

Editorial calendar, 76
Effective measurement, 134
Email alerts, Yelp reviews, 19
Employees
  community involvement,
    60–61
  LinkedIn search, 131
  participation, 87–89
  recruiting, 119–120
Engagement goals, 5–6
Engagement measures, 135
  Facebook, 138–139
  Google Analytics, 145
  Twitter, 140
Enhanced listings, review
    sites, 18

Entrepreneur's Organization
    (EO), 122
Events, website update, 109

Facebook, 5, 44–46
    advertising on, 52, 62,
        66–67
    business page, 66–67
    features, 65–66
    getting started, 63–69
    metrics, 136–139
    monitoring, 16, 17
    nerve center audit, 158t,
        158–159, 170
    profile mark, 1
    social media overview audit,
        153t, 154
    success tips, 69
Facebook Insights, 134
Facebook-only promotions,
    86, 87
Ferguson, Tim, 7, 54, 82
"Field of dreams" approach, 41
Fifth Street Public Market,
    Eugene, OR, 7–8, 52, 54,
        81, 141
Flickr, 4, 42
    social media overview audit,
        153t, 155
Focus group, online community
    as, 59
Focused messages, 74
Follower measures, 135
    Facebook, 137–138
    Google Analytics, 144–145
    Twitter, 140
Food blogging, 58

Foursquare, 4, 42, 111, 112
Friends, Facebook, 63–64
Friendster, 4

Gans, Rich and Kim, 8, 79, 80
Genre blogs, 34–35
Geolocation services, 42
Geosocial networks, 4, 110–112
Gillespie Florist, 8, 82, 83,
    109, 116
Goal setting
    blog, 38
    Facebook, 64
    social media, 5–6, 41–42, 62,
        164–165
Golden Gecko Garden Center,
    California, 9, 24, 47, 79,
        83, 117
Good conversations, 23–24
Google
    monitoring, 16–17
    search, 97, 99
    user-review sites, 19
Google AdWork Keyword
    Tool, 102
Google Alerts, 17, 47, 140
    industry news, 117
Google Analytics, 103,
    143–145, 147
Google Buzz, 4
Google Places
    local business, 20, 107,
        109–110
    setting up, 113–114
    success tips, 114
GorupM Search, 98
Gowalla, 4, 111, 112

Haenlein, Michael, 2
Hartwich, Lisa, 8, 27, 28, 50, 52, 86, 118, 119, 166
Hartwick's Kitchen Store, 8, 27, 28, 50, 52
Hashtag, Twitter, 94, 105
Hill, Napoleon, 121
HootSuite, Twitter tracking tool, 143
Host blog site, choosing, 35, 36t
Hotel Lucia, Portland, 10, 77, 125
HTML site map, 107, 108

Imagine Graphics, 1, 8, 50, 54, 59
Incentives, 52
Incoming links, 106
Information sharing, B2B, 116–118
Insider Pages, 4, 19, 107
  listening audit, 151
In-store promotion, 62
Interactions graph, Facebook, 137
Interactivity, 2, 55–57
  directional, 3
Internal links, 105
iPhones, check-ins, 110

Jaiku, 4
Jillian Bisinger Modern Photography, 7, 47, 52–53, 58, 74

Kaplan, Andreas, 2
Kennedy, William, 8, 46, 49, 88
Keotag, search, 21–22
Keywords
  audit, 157t
  content rich, 104

stuffing, 103
in URL, 104
King Estate Wineries, Oregon, 10, 118
Knowles, James, 72

Lake Street Creamery, Los Angeles, 7, 54, 82
Laughing Planet Café, The, Portland, 10, 24
Leads generation, B2B, 118
Leaf, Erica, 1, 8, 50, 54, 59, 87, 117–118, 142
LinkedIn, 4, 120, 128
  Answers section, 124, 130–131
  apps and features, 129–130
  company page, 129
  connection building, 129
  employee search, 130–131
  groups, 129–130
  job posting, 131–132
  profile, 128–129
  success tips, 132
Links
  adding, 105
  trading with other vendors, 109
LiveJournal, 3
Local search, 100–101
"Lo-So" (location social), 110
Lucas Oil Stadium, 8

Marche Restaurant, Eugene, 10, 77
MarketingProfs website, 133
Mason, Brian, 8, 45, 54, 115, 118, 166
Mastermind, 121–122

Matthews, Kelli, 7, 25, 51, 5, 166
Measurable, SMART goal
  methodology, 6, 134
Measurements
  blogging, 143–146
  Facebook, 136–139
  Twitter, 139–143
  types of 135
Media calendar, 75
Media metrics, 133
  blogging, 143–146
  Facebook, 136–139
  Twitter, 139–143
Mendenhall, Della, 8, 82, 83–84,
  97, 105, 109–110, 143–144
Mentions, placing in context,
  17–18
Mentions measures, 135
  Facebook, 139
  TweetMeme, 145–146
  Twitter, 141
Message management, 57–59
Microblogging, 4, 35
Miller, Paco, 8, 50, 75, 77,
  108, 111
Miller, Patty, 9, 27, 28, 46
Mobile services, 42
Monitoring services, 17–18
Monitoring tools, 22, 133, 146
Mountain Trek, 9, 45, 46, 84
Moveable Type, blog site, 36t
Multimedia sites, 4
MySpace, 4, 5, 42

Naked Pizza, 9, 31, 44, 45, 48
Naples Tomato in Naples, Florida,
  10, 77

Napoleon Hill Foundation, 122
Negative comments/reviews, 2,
  18, 24–29
  dealing with escalation, 29–31
  transparency, 26–27
"Nerve center"
  auditing, 156–158, 157t
  blog as, 47–48
  Facebook as, 44–46
  social media site, 43, 61, 155
  Twitter as, 46–47
Net Market Share, 99
Newsvine, 22
Niche blogging, 34–35
Niva, Brad, 9, 19, 31, 82, 87, 97,
  107, 110, 116, 117

Ogneva, Maria, 15
Online community building, 43
Online listening, 14, 23
  social media audit, 151–153,
  152t, 167
"Opinion leaders," 15–16
Opinion/user-review sites, 18–21
Organic search, 100
Osborn, Jennifer, 144
Outgoing links, 105
Outgoing links, nerve center audit,
  159, 163
"Overly managed," messages, 78

Pageview, Google Analytics,
  143, 144
Paid search, 100
Pelican Pub and Brewery, 9, 45
Performance over time, 135
Personal blogs, 33–34

Personal page, Facebook, 64–65
Photobucket, 4
Photography, 79–81
    signed release, 80n.1
Pitsenger, Trey, 9, 24, 47, 79,
    83, 117
Pollard, Daniel, 9, 45
Poloway, Janice (JP), 9, 45, 46, 84
Popular/less popular search term
    integration, 103
Portal, Facebook as, 49
Positive reviews
    commenting back, 24
    and promotion, 23
Positive word-of-mouth, 3
Presence, 52–55
    auditing, 152, 158
Prior pageview, Google
    Analytics, 144
Product/service of the week,
    website update, 109
Promotion
    in-store 62
    and positive reviews, 23
    timely, 76–78
Proprietary algorithm, search
    rating, 100
Purchasing followers, 138

Qaiku, 4
Qoola yogurt stores, Vancouver,
    10, 25, 27, 28, 42, 45, 46, 51,
    56, 58, 73–74, 87, 133, 141
Qualitative research, 134–135
Quantitative data, 134
Qwitter, Twitter tracking
    tool, 142

Rafting America, 116, 117
Realistic, SMART goal
    methodology, 6
Relevance, search rating, 100
Restaurant user-review sites, 20–21
Return on investment (ROI), 133
Retweeting, 24, 46, 94, 141
    social media overview audit,
    153t, 155
Review and opinion sites, 4
Robinson, "Utah"Dave, realtor, 9,
    26–27, 45, 48, 49, 51, 52, 57,
    83, 86, 116, 139
Roger Smith Hotel, New York,
    9–10, 25, 26, 31, 41, 46, 48,
    49, 81–82, 85, 88–89
Rogue Wilderness Adventures, 9,
    19, 31, 82, 87
Root folder, website, 104
Rotary club, 123
RRS feed, 49

Sales goals, 5
Search engine optimization
    (SE), 101
    audit, 156, 157t, 169
Search engines, 99
    ranking maintenance, 108
    social media, 21–23
    types, 100–101
Search optimization, 97–99,
    101–109
Search terms, 101–104
Service goals, 5
Service providers, 119
Sierra Trading Company,
    Cheyenne, 10, 56, 81

Simpson, Brian, 9
Site map, 107–108
  updating, 109
SKP-Popcorn, 8, 45, 54, 118
Small businesses, 2
  goal-setting, 6
SMART goal methodology,
  6, 134
Smith, Kevin, 29, 30, 31
"Social customers," 15
Social glue, 55, 72
  development, 73
Social listening, 15
Social media
  business-to-business use, 115
  communication, 71–72
  definition, 2
  return on investment
    (ROI), 133
  search engines, 21–23
  and search marketing, 98
  and word of mouth, 31–32
Social media audit, 150
  action plan, 164t,
    164–165, 171
  competitor list, 150–151
  "nerve center,"156–158, 157t,
    170, 171
  online listening audit, 151–153,
    152t, 167
  search engine optimization,
    156, 157t, 169
  sites overview, 153t,
    153–156, 168
  time period, 151
"Social media triumvirate," 42
Social Mention, 17, 23, 140

Social networking, 1
  and phones, 111
  services, 3
  site overview audit, 153t,
    153–156, 168
  sites, 4
Southwest Airlines, Dallas, 10, 29,
  30, 31
Special offers, 85–87
Specific, SMART goal
  methodology, 6
"Spiders," 99
  keyword stuffing avoidance, 104
Stobb, Justin, 9, 15, 74, 99, 104, 146
Storytelling
  community building, 75–76
  with passion, 74
  and social glue, 72
Surveys, 60
Sweet Flour Bakery, Toronto, 8,
  79, 80
Synching features, 123

Tattered Cover Bookstore, Denver,
  9, 27–28, 46
Testimonials, website update, 109
Thanking customers, 25, 56
Think and Grow Rich (Hill),
  121–122
Tia Juana's Beach Cantina, Maui, 8
Tia Juana's Long Bar and Grill,
  Irvine, CA, 8, 50
Time spent, Google Analytics, 145
Times, SMART goal
  methodology, 6
Transparency, negative reviews,
  26–27

Trip Advisor, 20, 31, 107
"Trust agents," 15
Trust building, 59
Tumblr, 4
"Tweak-out,"30, 31
Tweet, "retweet,"24
TweetBeep, 23, 134, 142
TweetDeck, 49
TweetMeme, 142–143
Twitter, 4, 46–47
    active users, 1, 91
    customizing, 93
    finding people, 93–94
    getting started, 91
    home page, 91–92
    lingo, 94–95
    link shortening, 95
    metrics, 139–143
    monitoring, 16, 17, 23
    nerve center audit, 160t,
        160–162, 170
    recruitment, 119
    social media overview audit,
        153t, 154–155
    success tips, 95
Twitterboard, 134
Twitter-only promotions,
    86, 87
TypePad, 3

Unique pageview, Google
    Analytics, 143
Unique visitors, Google
    Analytics, 144
Urbanspoon, 20–21
URL (Uniform Resource
    Locator), 104

User-generated content, 2, 84
User-review sites, 15, 18–21,
    107, 146
Users graph, Facebook, 136–137

Videos, 81–83
View points.com, 20
Visual images, 79–83
Vitrano, Robbie, 9, 31, 44, 45, 48,
    85, 97, 141
VVCs (very valuable
    customers), 57

Wallace, Adam, 9, 25, 26, 41, 46,
    48, 52, 57, 72, 82, 85,
    88–89, 136
WayBack Machine, 106
Website, social media overview
    audit, 153t, 154
Websites
    and blog integration, 104
    business, 98–99
    how found, 145
    updating, 108–109
Where the Locals East, 21
Word-of-mouth marketing, 2,
    31, 57
    comments, 24
    mentions as, 136
WordPress, 3. See also Blogging
    appearance customizing, 38
    blog creation, 35–36
    categories, 37
    information customizing, 38
    picture/video addition, 37
    post writing, 36–37
    website building, 98

WW Windows, California, 7, 102, 103

XML site map, 107, 108

YackTrack, 22
Yahoo
  local business, 20
  search, 99
Yammer, 4
Yellow Pages, 97, 111
Yelp, 4, 13, 19, 27, 28, 31, 107, 146

listening audit, 151
search, 97
YouTube, 4, 42, 82, 83
  social media overview audit, 153t, 155
Yu, Jesse, 10, 25, 27, 28, 42, 45, 46, 51, 56, 57, 58, 71, 73–74, 79, 87, 133, 141, 146, 166

Zagat, 21
Zide, 4
Zucca, Tony, 7, 47, 52–53, 58, 74, 80, 98, 103, 104

About the Authors

Steve O'Leary is the Chairman of O'Leary and Partners, an advertising agency in Orange County, CA. In his 35+ years in advertising, he has worked for over 20 different chains or franchise groups including Century 21, In-N-Out Burger, and Fantastic Sams Hair Salons. His client expertise also includes major brands such as Minute Maid, Miller Brewing, Subway, Scott Paper, Planters Nuts, and Bristol Myers. He is also a principal in Grabbing Green, a website devoted to helping small business owners with marketing and advertising issues they face in running their businesses. With Kim Sheehan, he has written two other books on small business marketing. He is a highly regarded speaker at various industry events and client conventions and has been a guest lecturer at numerous universities. Steve is a proud University of Oregon alumnus. He is an inductee to the Hall of Achievement for the School of Journalism and Communication at the UO and a current member of the Journalism Advancement Council.

Kim Sheehan is Professor of Advertising at the School of Journalism and Communication at the University of Oregon. Before joining the academy, she worked for over a dozen years at major advertising agencies in Chicago and Boston. She received the BS from Northwestern University, the MBA from Boston University, and the PhD from the University of Tennessee. With Steve O'Leary, she is a principal in Grabbing Green. She has authored or coauthored seven books and over two dozen academic articles concerning advertising and new media.

Sterling Lentz is the lead project manager at online marketing agency Adpearance in Portland, Oregon. There he leverages an arsenal of interactive channels to help small and medium-sized businesses excel in traditional marketing and emerging online media. Lentz is an alumnus of the School of Journalism and Robert D. Clark Honors College at the University of Oregon.